cork
design guide:
building a new house
in the countryside

by Colin Buchanan and Partners Ltd
and Mike Shanahan + Associates, Architects

Published by Cork County Council 2003

Reprinted with corrections February 2004

A joint production of the Cork County Architect and the Planning Policy Unit.

Cork County Council would be pleased to receive any comments on the contents and utility of the guide, and especially any suggestions as to how it could be improved.

Any comments should be sent to:
> Planning Policy Unit
> Bishopstown House
> Cork County Council
> Model Farm Road, Cork

Copies can be obtained from :
> Planning Department
> Cork County Council
> Model Business Park
> Model Farm Road
> Cork
> Tel: 021 4867006

ISBN 0 9525 86940

Printed by
City Print Ltd.,
Carrigrohane Road,
Victoria Cross,
Cork

1

2

foreword

If you are thinking of buying a rural site, involved in selecting or designing a house for a particular site, or just interested in County Cork's heritage and future development, then this guide is for you.

The Guide is intended to make it easier to gain planning permission for those proposing to build, renovate or extend individual houses in rural County Cork. It does this by making clearer what Cork County Council and its planning officers and town architects are seeking, and explaining how choices about the site and the design can make all the difference to the success of a planning application and the completed house.

Other aims of the Guide are to

- stimulate debate about design;
- foster greater consistency in planning decision making;
- inform and inspire applicants, builders, designers and planners;
- and conserve and enhance the Cork landscape and environment.

This Guide does not cover matters such as whether a proposed house is permissible in a particular area of the County, or in what circumstances. For answers on these questions refer to the County (or Town) Development Plan and any Local Area Plan, or contact the Area Planner (or Town Architect). Neither is this Guide intended to specifically address housing development in villages and towns, or development other than houses in rural areas, though there is much in the Guide that may be of assistance to anyone undertaking such development.

It is unlikely that everyone would agree with all the examples and suggestions made in the Guide. Hopefully, people will think about and discuss how and why their views differ or agree with those in the Guide, and in this way the quality and profile of the debate will be raised.

It should be clear to anyone reading and looking at the examples in this Guide that the Council is not seeking to have all houses look the same. Rather, the Guide encourages the imaginative and radical as well as the tried and tested, provided they complement their surroundings. It does this by promoting an understanding of key design principles and the characteristics of Cork heritage and landscape.

Good design is not just a matter of taste. There are identifiable techniques and characteristics which will enable someone to make a house more efficient, more practical, and better related to its surroundings. This Guide provides an outline of these methods and considerations. If it can contribute to today's rural houses being regarded in the future as good places to live, and good things to look at, then it will have been a success.

contents

foreword   3

introduction   7

part one - careful site selection   12

part two - well considered site layout   26

part three - appropriate house design   52

part four- good construction   74

part five - worked example   102

appendices   119

    addressing the deep plan house   120
    trees and shrubs   123
    bibliography   125
    photo & design credits   127
    acknowledgements & accreditation   130

introduction

Few could argue that the countryside of Cork is one of the County's most valuable assets. It has an economic value, not just for its productive yield in the traditional industries of agriculture, forestry and fishing, but also for its very real value to the modern tourist industry. The latter is increasingly replacing the former as the anchor of the region's prosperity. A more obvious value lies simply in its scenic beauty, natural diversity and the pleasant, clean environment it provides for all of us to enjoy.

Cork County Council commissioned this guide in response to the pace of change now occurring across the County. Cork, just like the rest of Ireland, is currently experiencing an economic boom unlike any other in its history. Prosperity in the housing market has generated increasing pressure on rural parts of the County to absorb and provide for increasing levels of growth. More rural houses have been constructed since the boom of the mid-1990s than ever before in Cork's post-famine history. As the largest county in Ireland, with a substantial coastline of over 1,100 km, the challenge is to direct and manage this change to ensure that new housing development is in harmony with the outstanding environmental qualities of the County. These qualities include a very distinctive built heritage in rural architecture, a heritage as important to our cultural identity as our language, music and literature.

This guide is intended to assist applicants to gain planning permission for new homes by highlighting the key issues that should be addressed at an early stage in the house design process. It is aimed at all of those who are involved in the process of building a new house in rural Cork – the householder, designer, builder and planning officer. It is perhaps regrettable that there has been a general acceptance in recent times of extremely unimaginative standards of domestic 'rural' house design across the County. Responsibility for standards rests with each of these parties and in particular with those who prepare and submit plans on the public's behalf. What is important now is that this joint responsibility is recognised and that all parties make an effort to restore some direction to the evolution of modern domestic rural architecture in the County. Those most qualified to lead this change are the architectural profession, many of whom have generously contributed illustrations of their work to this document. Cork County Council and the authors strongly urge those seeking to build a new house in the countryside to consider the advantages of obtaining qualified architectural advice.

This Design Guide is first of a series which will gives effect to objective ENV 5-8 of the County Development Plan 2003. The guide does not purport to explain the Development Plan or the Building Regulations, and does not alter the need to have regard to that Plan and to comply with the Building Regulations.

approach

This guide will illustrate an approach to location that reflects the incredibly diverse landscape types that stretch across Ireland's largest county, from its uplands and agricultural hinterlands in the north to its busy coastline and island communities in the south and west. Advice on siting and layout will be dominated by the age-old considerations of shelter and blending with the landscape, with some practical thoughts on planning for privacy, play space, sewage treatment, access and respect for one's neighbours.

On the issue of design, the guide will on the one hand illustrate good, exciting, site specific contemporary houses which have been skilfully conceived and executed on appropriate sites (most often involving qualified architects), and on the other highlight the importance of simplicity, restraint, proportion and quality of materials. These are all key characteristics which make the architectural inheritance of Cork rural buildings so distinctive. Elements of Irish rural houses are examined and regional characteristics of the County explored. Some elements, such as windows, chimneys and doors need to be examined in detail, as these are all critical to successful rural design. However, the emphasis is not with the past but with the future. This guide aims to inspire the best in modern, contemporary Irish rural design. A design tradition that is Irish in origin; confident, assertive, artistic and a worthy contribution to Cork's future built heritage.

What does this guide aim to achieve?

- Better designed houses for people to live in;
- Better located houses to look after the appearance of the countryside;
- More thoughtful siting of houses to make them warmer and more comfortable places to live;
- Cheaper and more efficient houses to heat in the future through the use of energy saving technologies and renewable sources of energy in accordance with insulation requirements of the Building Regulations;
- The promotion of contemporary Irish design and the regional characteristics of Cork architecture;
- An easier understanding of how to gain planning permission by making better applications, with well-designed houses on carefully selected sites.

this guide will emphasise:

Stewardship/Guardianship - Each one of us has a responsibility as steward of the countryside not just to preserve heritage, but to create a heritage for the enjoyment of future generations. The building of a new house in the countryside should be a positive addition to the rural environment and not appear incongruous with, or detract from, its surroundings.

A Sense of Place and Community - Much of the character and quality of the Cork countryside derives from the range of traditional buildings and their use of local materials. These buildings are part of Cork's heritage and regional identity. Whilst not advocating an imitation of the past, new buildings should reflect the dynamics of their location, the availability of local materials and the built character of what has gone before.

Contemporary Rural Living and Lifestyles - Adaptation to modern living and lifestyles must be an essential component of any new design. This guide aims to offer a more exciting and sympathetic alternative to the suburban style of many new rural homes.

The Long Term - A new dwelling permanently alters the landscape, therefore a new building needs to be designed and constructed with a view to the long term implications of its impact on its surroundings. Buildings should be durable, capable of future adaptation, and integrate fully with the local landscape.

Innovation and Quality - Striking a balance between prescription and innovation, tradition and contemporary is not always an easy task. Good design respects and learns from what has gone before and interprets traditional forms and materials in the contemporary context. Innovative design is a welcome addition to the rural countryside, but only if expertly and sensitively handled.

Affordability - Good design does not equate to expensive design. It is just as possible to have a well-designed affordable home in a rural landscape, as it is to have a badly designed costly dwelling. This guide recognises that not all applicants wishing to build in a rural locality can afford to pay a designer. However by sticking to the general rules of simplicity and modesty it is possible to construct a well-designed, affordable "dream home".

13   14   15   16

17

good planning & design

This guide is laid out to take you through the following considerations when preparing to submit a planning application. These considerations are not sequential but need to be addressed in parallel to produce the most favourable outcome. Each aspect is designed to assist you to submit a successful proposal for a new house in the Cork countryside. These considerations are summarised in the following key points:

 careful site selection Check location issues in the County Development Plan. Seek out good 'Natural Sites', which will reduce the impact of new houses. Choose sites offering shelter, privacy and good orientation, i.e. allow more extensive south-facing glazing unseen from neighbouring roads, with existing features if possible. Recognise that prominent or sensitive sites will require more care and skilful handling. Avoid sites that will entail removal of attractive roadside hedgerows, trees, etc.

 well considered site layout Address prominence, shelter, passive solar gain, privacy and impact issues with various house locations, types and orientations before finalising site selection or house design. Maximise the benefit of existing site features. Ensure the house appears to sit down into the site. Address functional engineering issues in parallel, such as safe access, drainage, etc. Reduce the openness of the site by breaking it down into different areas. Locate cars out of sight. Minimise green baize lawn areas.

 appropriate house design The site and the development of a good layout should inform the shape and height of a new house. Keep the shape of the house very simple. Minimise modelling of the 'front' facade. Develop the house design to incorporate attributes of rural houses of the area, paying particular attention to good proportioning. Cork rural houses tend to be deceptively simple and well-mannered. Always ask if the house proposed is appropiate to the site context, if not seek an alternative site or different house design. Be aware that larger houses need large sites and/or massing needs to be simply broken down.

 landscape design In parallel with site and house design, the landscape 'design' of the site should endeavour to link the new house with the countryside around it. House, garden and landscape must be designed as a unit if the house is to achieve a strong link to the land. Differing types of countryside will result in different appropriate responses to the landscape. Aim to achieve naturalistic planting effects using predominately indigenous/local species and groupings. Buffer the house from the road or public view to reduce impact and leave the existing roadside/ hedgerow/ boundary intact wherever possible. Make areas for plants to grow against the new house. Minimise the extent of mown lawn areas.

 good construction 'The devil is in the detail'. Traditional detailing gives many clues as to how new houses can settle more happily with older neighbouring houses, irrespective of style. Irish rural houses traditionally rely solely on attractive proportioning, careful use of colour and quality of materials for their success. More often there was substance to what was built. For example houses near the coast look as if they were built for hurricane climates with minimal eaves and verge, etc. Avoid white plastic and 'add-on frills' wherever possible.

A checklist is provided at the end of each section to alert you to potential problems and to guide you along. The worked example at the end shows you exactly what the planner will need in order to consider and assess your application.
It is important to note that, in all instances, your building must comply with current Building Regulations.

part one
site selection

- Check the development plan
- Reading the landscape
- Choosing where to build
- Assessing a site's potential
- Linking with the land
- Summary & Checklist

site selection

The successful siting of a new house in the countryside requires care and consideration. It should involve an analysis of the impact the house will have on the appearance of the land, the impact it will have on the comfort of its occupants, together with practical considerations of connecting to power, water and roads. The landscapes of the County differ so much that the response to location will reflect local circumstances and local settlement patterns. This section helps you to identify landscape characteristics and gives advice on how you can work with these characteristics to integrate your new home into the very fabric of the countryside.

A well sited house will save you money because it will be well sheltered, retain more heat and use less energy.

The aim is to ensure that new development appears visually integrated and sympathetic with its surrounding landscape rather than imposed upon it.

A dwelling badly sited will alter the character and appearance of the landscape, often setting a poor precedent for future development to follow. However, **where siting is carefully considered**, it is possible to construct a dwelling that not only contributes to the character of the landscape but which sets high standards in terms of siting, location, and design, and which both respects and reflects local traditions. It will be oriented to face south for warmth, and be landscaped to provide shelter from the prevailing wind and be situated to provide privacy from the road.

When choosing a site check the Cork County Development Plan, and any Local Area Plan for the locality, in particular for:

- Policies restricting/permitting development in certain areas eg. Greenbelt, Coastal Areas, Rural Housing Control Zone etc
- Scenic Amenity Maps - scenic routes and scenic landscapes;
- Heritage maps - Natural Heritage Areas (NHA), Special Protection Areas (SPA) and candidate Special Area of Conservation (SAC) and Areas of Geological Interest;
- Landscape Character Maps;
- Archaeology policies, the Record of Protected Structures and conservation policies.

If your site falls within any of these areas take advice from the Council Planning Department before proceeding.

reading the landscape

Mountains	Fertile Plain of Blackwater Valley	Fissured Marginal and Forested Rolling Upland	River and Reservoir Valleys	Ridged, Peaked & Forested Upland
• Derrynasaggart				
• Ballyhoura	• Banteer	• Boggeragh	• Inishcarra	• Inchigeelagh
• Nagles	• Mallow	• Mullaghareirk	• Coachford	• Millstreet
	• Fermoy		• Macroom	

As the largest county in Ireland, the landscapes we have in Cork vary greatly. It is a rich and diverse landscape. Landscape types range from the rolling hills, valleys and scrub of the farmland and moorlands of north Cork, through the low-lying flatlands, rivers and lakes of the central area, to the uplands and valleys of the east. This contrasts with the rocky and rugged ridges and peninsulas to the west, particularly along the Beara peninsula, and the patchwork of fertile coastline mixed with estuarine mudflats along the southern coastal region. Also, one must not forget the multitude of islands off the west coast of the County, with their myriad stone walls marking out field boundaries.

Geologically the County is comprised of two rock types: predominantly old red sandstone, with a smattering of carboniferous limestone more dominant in the south and east, both of which influence the raw materials used for construction. Each of these landscapes require different considerations, particularly when selecting a site for a building platform. A regional variation in housing design occurs within the County, related to the East/West regional variation throughout Ireland. Variations in regional housing design were a direct response to the local environment.

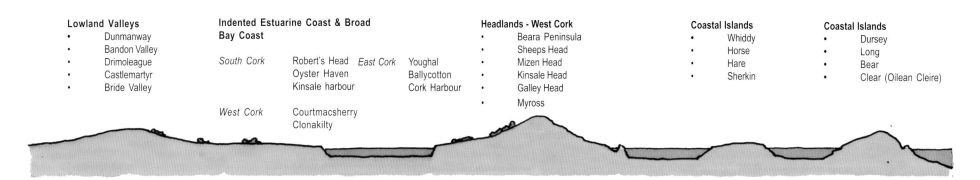

Lowland Valleys	Indented Estuarine Coast & Broad Bay Coast			Headlands - West Cork	Coastal Islands	Coastal Islands
• Dunmanway				• Beara Peninsula	• Whiddy	• Dursey
• Bandon Valley				• Sheeps Head	• Horse	• Long
• Drimoleague	*South Cork*	Robert's Head *East Cork*	Youghal	• Mizen Head	• Hare	• Bear
• Castlemartyr		Oyster Haven	Ballycotton	• Kinsale Head	• Sherkin	• Clear (Oilean Cleire)
• Bride Valley		Kinsale harbour	Cork Harbour	• Galley Head		
				• Myross		
	West Cork	Courtmacsherry				
		Clonakilty				

Throughout the County, buildings were orientated to make best use of shelter and sun, using natural features such as the lie of the land combined with hedgerows and shelterbelts to best protect them from the elements. Small farm holdings and clachans were more common in the west of the County, as was the long house.

The coastal islands, most of which lie off the west or southwest coastline, were more exposed and therefore dwellings tended to be single storey with west-facing gable ends for shelter. These included Congested Districts Board housing such as rural labourers' cottages, and were essentially improved versions of traditional dwellings, perpetuating the lobby entrance but replacing the hipped roofs with gables and the thatch with slates. Almost all of the houses on Long Island, south-west Cork, were rebuilt by the Congested Districts Board, using two-storeyed farmhouses and small houses with attic bedrooms. In the north and east of the County, with its rolling hills and valleys, the hipped roof was more prevalent. Walls were traditionally mud and stone and roofs were often thatched, reflecting the agricultural nature of settlement. From the 19th century slate replaced thatch as the dominant roof material. Corrugated iron was also used to replace thatch.

choosing where to build

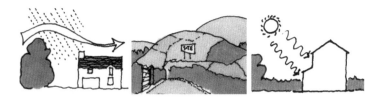

Having considered the nature of the landscape in which we want to build, we then need to choose where in that landscape it is best to locate a new house. Two factors should dominate this decision - shelter and orientation towards the sun. Some sites require different responses to others. Less sensitive sites can take much more individualistic houses, whereas more prominent or sensitive sites require greater skill and care.

A great deal can be learnt from observation of traditional methods of site layout, which appear more integrated within the landscape. These involve making use of natural tucks in the landscape, sheltered areas beside woodland, working with gradients and not against them, and generally choosing locations which avoid the worst effects of the wind and the rain. Distance to local facilities should be a critical factor in selecting a site. Try to choose a site that is close to work, school and shops etc. to avoid the need to travel too far for daily journeys

avoid exposure & prominence

- Study the alignment and orientation of older houses in the area e.g. the traditional alignment of houses - gable to wind/west to maximise shelter and reduce exposure

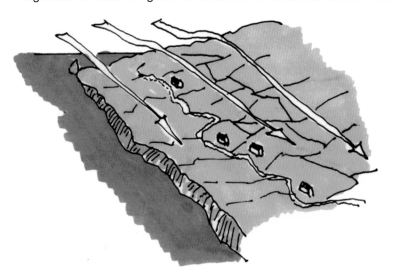

• Avoid building on prominent, unsheltered hillside location

• Avoid building on ridges - prominent, exposed with huge heat losses in winter

seek shelter & integration ..use natural elements to your advantage

• Where possible use the natural backdrop of trees/ shelter belt. **Note**: deciduous planting to the south will give summer shade and winter light

• Huddle of buildings in lee of knoll

• House sited in a hollow using the hillside for shelter

• House built in a 'tuck' on a headland

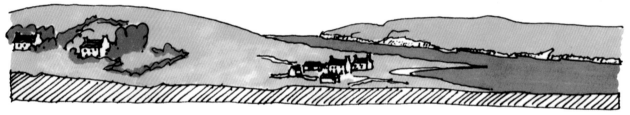

• Inland sites using tree cover

• Coastal-clustering clachan

assessing a site's potential ...a possible good site and three responses

The site is sloping southwards, has trees as a backdrop, shelter from the hillside, hedgerows to the front and easy access to services at the roadside.

This exercise aims to illustrate how an applicant buying a site, or a farmer selling a site, might consider some typical responses which often create planning difficulties. By looking at the same piece of land with a slight change in approach in site layout and house design we can achieve a much more satisfactory result.

Corner of a Farm Holding

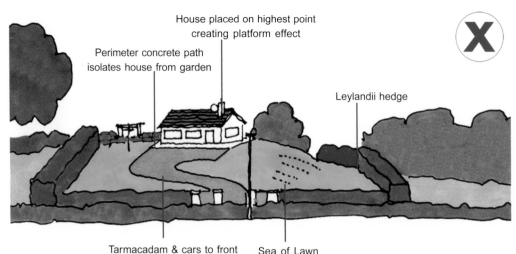

House placed on highest point creating platform effect

Perimeter concrete path isolates house from garden

Leylandii hedge

Tarmacadam & cars to front

Sea of Lawn

The `Drop-in' Bungalow

A typical response of the 70s & 80s to avoid

- House positioned on the most elevated and exposed part of the site
- Pattern book bungalow isolated from the landscape by concrete path and manicured garden
- Suburban treatment of house and garden with no use of 'natural' landscaping
- Hedgerows removed and replaced with Leylandii hedging
- Lack of enclosure
- Absence of privacy
- Cars to the front

The 90s Approach

Big house too close to road, full impact presentation

- House positioned to be seen. Large in scale, dominant within the local landscape
- No shelter or link with the landscape - exposed and buffered by the weather, no enclosure or privacy to the garden areas
- Sea of green lawn and tarmac, cars to the front
- Poor use of materials and detailing, lots of plastic and imitation stone facings
- A platform has to be cut and/or built up because the footprint of the house does not relate to the contours of the land.

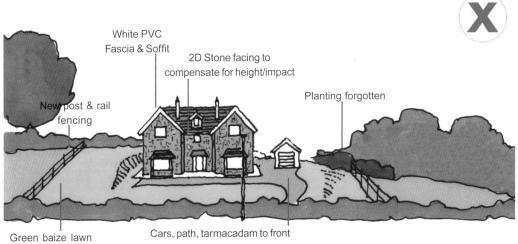

White PVC Fascia & Soffit

2D Stone facing to compensate for height/impact

Planting forgotten

New post & rail fencing

Green baize lawn

Cars, path, tarmacadam to front

The All-Show Clunky House

Rural Cork 2000s

Rural type house & site layout, links it with countryside & neighbours

- Most sheltered part of the site selected
- House orientated to maximise daylight and solar gain
- House set down into landscape and well linked to it
- Set back from the road and retaining the frontage hedgerows
- The massing of the house is broken down and follows the contour of the hills without the need for a platform
- Garden areas are secluded and private
- Modern comfortable home that blends with its setting

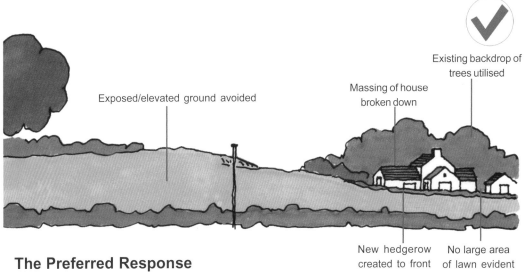

Existing backdrop of trees utilised

Massing of house broken down

Exposed/elevated ground avoided

New hedgerow created to front

No large area of lawn evident

The Preferred Response

linking with the land

A good site, from a planning viewpoint, might be defined as one which easily allows a new house to settle into and integrate with its surroundings. Too many new houses appear as if they've been lifted from a town suburb and simply placed on top of a rocky hillside. The secret is to work with the landscape and not against it. Keep as many hedgerows, trees, and stone walls as you can. Place the driveway to the side or rear. Keep expansive green lawns under control and plant the garden close to the house.

- Leave existing roadside hedgerows and ditches intact as much as possible;
- Avoid car parking to the 'front' of the house, i.e. between the house and the road. This will often mean making entrance courtyards or locating the 'front door' to the side or rear of the house, as seen from the road;
- Use contours of original site to soften the setting of the house;
- Try to retain at least two, preferably three, existing boundaries (either natural hedgerows or stone walls) to soften visual impact of the house;
- Pull paths a couple of feet away from the house to allow zone for planting contact with the house;
- Allow the garden to run up to/meet with the house in places, greatly enhancing its connection with the site. Avoid encircling house fully with paths;
- Use hedges, walls and planting close to the house to reduce its impact and assist in connecting it with its site;
- Plant and/or contour the site where necessary to maximise sheltering the house;
- Reduce/minimise the hard landscape zone about the house, isolating it from the garden which reinforces a 'platform' effect;
- Avoid isolating a house on a platform on the site surrounded by a sea of mown lawn;
- Use materials of the locality, e.g. stone and pea gravel from nearby quarries, etc. Avoid black tarmacadam driveways, brick 'features' which are out of context, or manufactured looking materials, such as some pre-cast concrete products;
- Avoid asphalt finishes and decorative lamps illuminating driveways as these are not suited to rural locations.

Alien 'Helicopter Drop-in' effect to house + site

House isolated, cars to front, sea of lawn

Attractive roadside wall, contouring, natural enclosure

House isolated, urban boundaries, no buffering

Rural road and wall, no concrete path, house anchored

House isolated from site, site isolated from the landscape

House + site linked to countryside

23

summary & checklist
site selection

have you?

Described the important characteristics of the site? ☐

Found a site in the optimum location in terms of visual impact - i.e avoided a prominent position? ☐

Found a site that provides shelter from prevailing winds and landscaping - i.e. avoided the ridge line and found a site with a natural back drop? ☐

Found a site with the appropriate aspect to maximise the sunlight? ☐

Found a site where at least two but preferably three existing natural boundaries can be retained (e.g. existing hedgerows, walls or woodland)? ☐

Found a site that allows safe access without removal of roadside boundaries? ☐

Created privacy for the proposed dwelling? ☐

Assessed alternative sites for their suitability? ☐

part two
well considered
site layout

20 things every house should consider

Orientation and mapping the sunpath

Study the options

Dealing with contours

Garden design

Creating new boundaries

New planting

Making an entrance

Summary & Checklist

site layout

The purpose of this section is to illustrate that by observing traditional principles and some common sense, we can achieve development that is more sympathetic and integrated into the surrounding landscape. This will ultimately enhance the energy performance of the dwelling making it cheaper to run and more comfortable to live in. The principles contained within this section should be considered in conjunction with the principles of site selection:

• Take advantage of natural light and heat	• Identify the wind direction and sun path throughout the year
• Orientate the dwelling to reduce exposure to the wind	• Design to link with the landscape
• Consider new site and boundary treatment carefully	

Examples of site layout designed as a direct response to the existing contours and natural features

38   39   40

20 things a rural house should consider...

The proper planning of a modern rural home requires that thought be given to a broad range of items. Too often only the practical servicing items get attention and the rest are ignored. Yet we need garden and amenity areas effectively screened from the road where we can enjoy our home and allow our children to play safely, as well as work and refuse areas that are well hidden from public view. Energy efficiency and environmental concerns need to play a greater role in the design and layout of our homes. There is a link between the desirability of reducing CO_2 emissions and the demands of, for instance, the role of parents as a `taxi' service for their children's school and other activities. Distance to local services must therefore be a critical factor when planning the construction of a new home. Try to choose a site that is close to work, the shops and where the children go to school, to avoid the need to travel too far for daily journeys. Also try to strike a balance between shelter from the wind and exposure to the sun. By simply orientating the house to maximise solar gain it is possible to reduce fuel consumption and create a brighter home.

When the 20 things illustrated on the facing page are not given thorough consideration, the result, as illustrated below, left gives rise to an impoverished layout with no screening, privacy or shelter. Alternatively, if issues are thought about at the outset they will influence the type of site selected and lead to a much improved proposal, as illustrated below right. The following section of this guide will take you through the factors that should be considered when designing a rural home.

1 Local facilities	✓	
2 Prominence	X	
3 Energy	X	
4 Sun	X	
5 Shelter	X	
6 Access	✓	
7 Power	✓	
8 Water	✓	
9 Telecoms	✓	
10 Drainage	✓	
11 Fuel /Storage	X	
12 Refuse	X	
13 Work Area	X	
14 Recycling	X	
15 TV & Satellite	✓	
16 Parking	✓	
17 Privacy	X	
18 Safety	X	
19 Clothes/ Line	X	
20 Garden Amenity	X	

8/20 - Poor solution

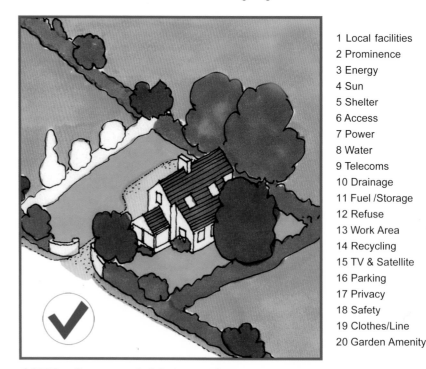

1 Local facilities	✓
2 Prominence	✓
3 Energy	✓
4 Sun	✓
5 Shelter	✓
6 Access	✓
7 Power	✓
8 Water	✓
9 Telecoms	✓
10 Drainage	✓
11 Fuel /Storage	✓
12 Refuse	✓
13 Work Area	✓
14 Recycling	✓
15 TV & Satellite	✓
16 Parking	✓
17 Privacy	✓
18 Safety	✓
19 Clothes/Line	✓
20 Garden Amenity	✓

20/20 - Successful integration

Distance to local facilities

Prominence/Impact

Energy Conservation

Sun

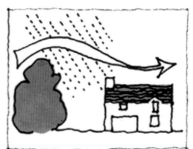
Shelter

Safe access

Power

Water

Telecommunications

Drainage

Fuel Storage Area

Refuse storage area

Tools/work area

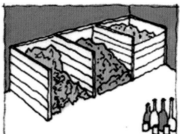
Recycling area

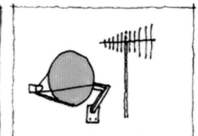
T.V. Receivers

Cars turning/parking

Privacy

Safe kids play area

Clothes drying area

Garden amenity areas/veg etc.

orientation
... capture the sun's free energy

Examine the site's exposure to the natural elements, particularly the sun and prevailing winds. By identifying the wind direction and sun's path throughout the year, the dwelling can be orientated to reduce exposure to the wind and take advantage of a natural source of light and heat - maximising from passive solar gain. This will significantly improve the energy performance of the dwelling. A good site layout is one that successfully manages to resolve the often conflicting considerations affecting on the way a house should be orientated - views, the sun, shelter, privacy, minimising impact and so on.

- Consider the best vantage points from the established sheltered positions to maximise views and prospects from the dwelling so that the orientation of the dwelling can then be determined - sometimes it may be necessary to rotate a house on the site so that its impact can be minimised. Also note that it is possible to capture a view without orientating the whole house towards it, e.g. by placing windows in gable ends
- Be careful in managing the conflict between privacy and glazed frontages facing the road

Highly glazed south elevations present problems where they are seen from the road

Highly glazed south elevations possible where topography or substantial existing tree cover offers screening

Appropriate solid looking appearance achieved by selecting site with northerly presentation to road

Use of glazed walls to maximise natural light and heat - most suited to private rear elevations

Carefully sited eco-house near Bandon (Photo 43) - designed entirely to maximise solar gain and be energy efficient. Not suited to every location but well sited here within 1 hectare of woodland

map the sunpath

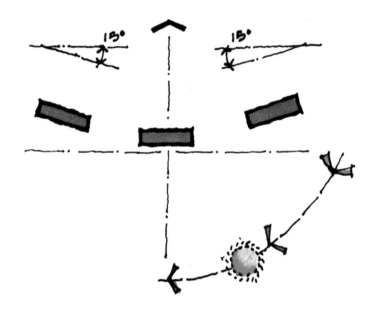

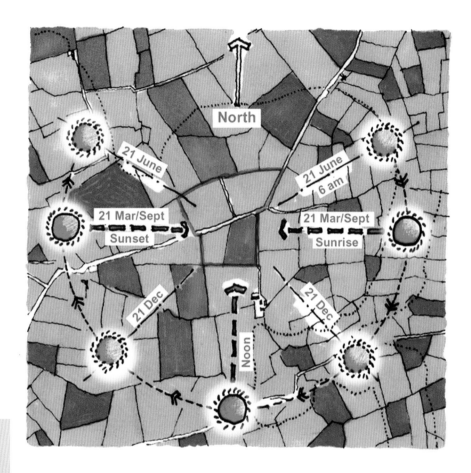

The sun's position changes throughout the seasons

30% energy savings can be achieved if a house is orientated within 15° of south, providing its main living spaces are arranged to avail of the passive solar gains. Cork County Council's Energy Agency are able to provide free impartial advice on issues relating to energy efficiency when planning a site layout and designing a house. They can be contacted at:

Spa House
Mallow, Co Cork
tel: 022 43610
fax: 022 43678
e-mail: mallowre@indigo.ie

Eco-architecture and energy efficient design is a specialist skill. Refer to the Royal Institute of Architects of Ireland for practitioners in this field of design.

Study your landholding carefully and select a site that gives you the best orientation to the sun, whilst also affording shelter from the weather, particularly prevailing winds. Choose a site where can you best achieve the 20 things identified on the previous pages. For example in the illustration above, choosing the site to the south of the road would enable a solid aspect (front of the house) to be presented to the road and a sunny, sheltered, private rear garden.
Options for selecting the best site are examined overleaf.

search for the best site option

Some sites are easier to work with than others. In order to illustrate the implications of different site choices, the illustration opposite shows 8 potential sites located around a hill. A road winds around the hill with sites either above the road (on a higher slope) or below the road. The following pages outline the constraints and possibilities of each of the sites. All of the sites are laid out following common objectives to accommodate the "20 things" referred to earlier (see pages 30 & 31). Each site layout seeks to resolve privacy/screening conflicts: avoiding large glazed areas facing the road and discreetly locating car parking and utility areas. The layouts seek to break down the site, reducing extensive unnatural lawn areas, to develop more natural and rural-type gardens.

The following factors influence the siting of the house:
1.   In every instance, the location of the septic tank/percolation area, determined by the fall across the site, dictates the position of the house;
2.   Sites accessed on the outside of a bend, i.e. in this diagram below the road, will generally more easily meet the local authority entrance requirements noted later in this section. Sites on the inside of a bend, i.e. in this instance those sites depicted above the road, tend to have greater difficulty meeting entrance requirements;
3.   The orientation, without exception, is dictated by low energy design objectives maximising on passive solar heating gains by orientating the house to the south, and sheltering from the prevailing southwesterly winds.
4.   All the sites have at least 2 existing mature boundaries which are retained and utilised to minimise the visual impact of the new development.
5.   Due to the terrain, some sites are naturally easier than others to site a house. In general, although not always, the sites above the road will be more prominent and therefore require more careful consideration with respect to house siting and screening. Privacy is affected by the orientation of the site. Sites B and E present the greatest difficulties as a south-facing house will be facing the road, therefore there will be conflicts in terms of privacy. Also sites with the southwest side facing the road will have evening patios facing the road (i.e. D and H).

The final site layout will depend on the existing site conditions as you find them. In the illustration opposite, sites A, C and F are the easiest to work with in terms of privacy, glazing, orientation and so forth.

45   46   47

Site Selection Guide: The constraints and possibilities of each of the sites below are set out in the following pages.

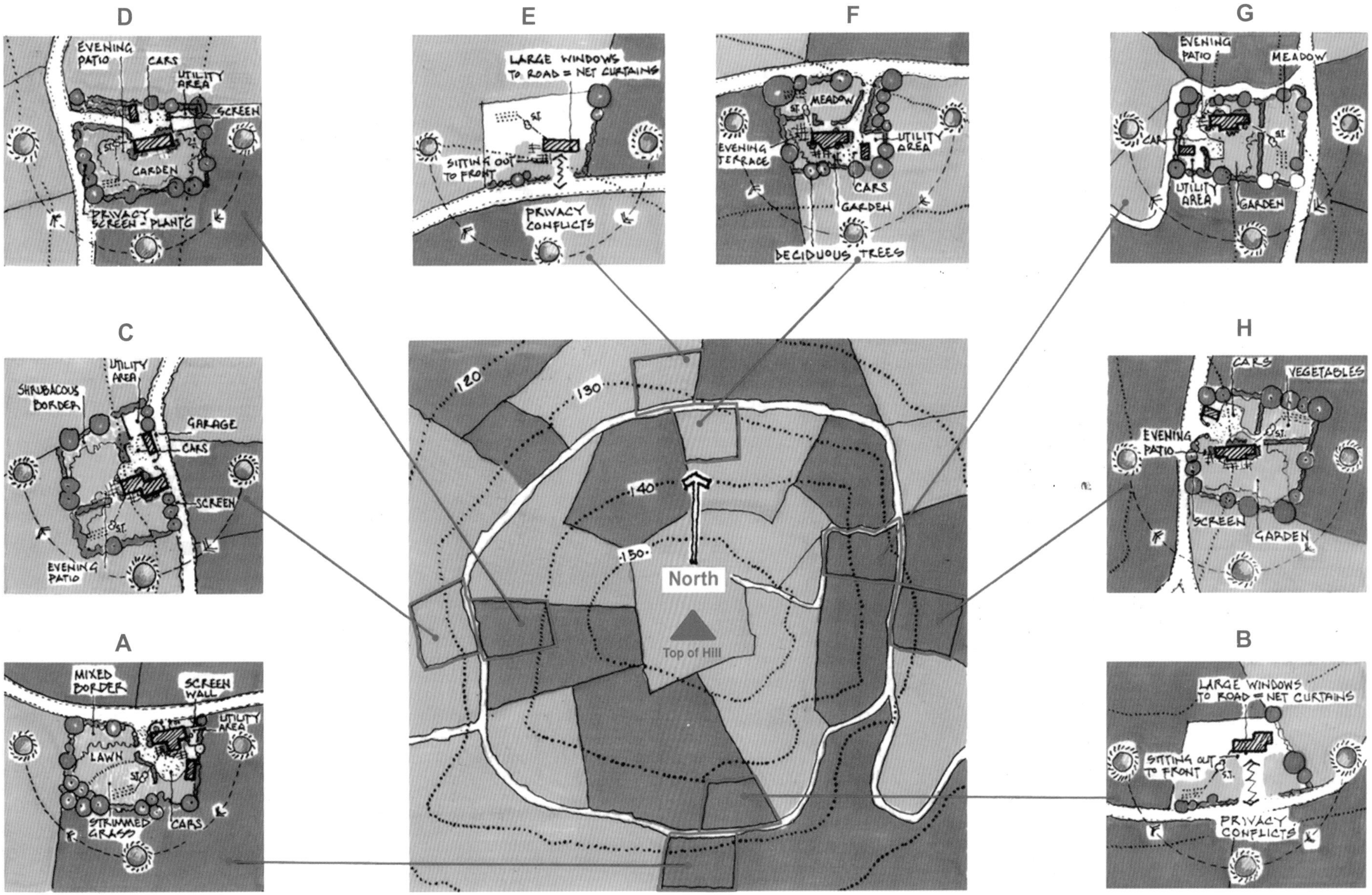

D

EVENING PATIO
CARS
UTILITY AREA
SCREEN
ST.
GARDEN
PRIVACY SCREEN PLANTS

E

LARGE WINDOWS TO ROAD = NET CURTAINS
ST.
SITTING OUT TO FRONT
PRIVACY CONFLICTS

F

MEADOW
ST.
EVENING TERRACE
UTILITY AREA
CARS
GARDEN
DECIDUOUS TREES

G

EVENING PATIO
MEADOW
CAR
ST.
UTILITY AREA
GARDEN

C

SHRUBACOUS BORDER
UTILITY AREA
GARAGE
CARS
SCREEN
ST.
EVENING PATIO

H

CARS
VEGETABLES
EVENING PATIO
ST.
SCREEN
GARDEN

A

MIXED BORDER
SCREEN WALL
UTILITY AREA
LAWN
ST.
STRIMMED GRASS
CARS

B

LARGE WINDOWS TO ROAD = NET CURTAINS
SITTING OUT TO FRONT
ST.
PRIVACY CONFLICTS

120
130
140
150
North
Top of Hill

Eight sites surrounding a hill

A SOUTH FACING SLOPE – Site Below Road

- Fall across site enables septic tank to be located to the rear of the house, further away from the road
- House is set back from road with boundary treatment, which also effectively screens utility area from dwelling and road and enables maximum privacy in the layout and arrangement of the outdoor sitting area
- Garage is located to the rear of the dwelling and thus both the garage and car court are effectively screened from the road

Conclusion: Potentially a good site and attractive site layout.

B SOUTH FACING SLOPE - Site Above Road

- Fall across site requires the septic tank and percolation area to be located to the front of the house, near the road
- To maximise sun and daylight the house needs its largest windows to the roadside, and the location of the outdoor sitting area to the front of the dwelling nearer the road, both of which conflict with privacy

Conclusion: Although this site is south-facing, it is not such a good site as large windows with net curtains will be necessary on elevation facing road to maximise daylight yet facilitate privacy.

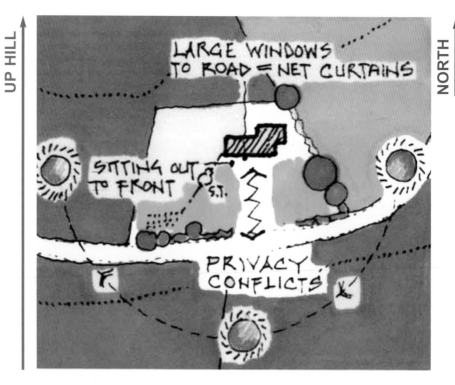

C WEST FACING SLOPE – Site Below Road

- Fall across site places septic tank and percolation areas at lower area, furthest away from road while house and garage are positioned in traditional Cork relationship with road – i.e. gable on and lengthways respectively at road edge
- Existing boundaries used in part to screen off utility area
- Garage location screens car court from road
- Layout of house and site affords maximum privacy to evening sitting out area

Conclusion: potentially a good site and attractive site layout.

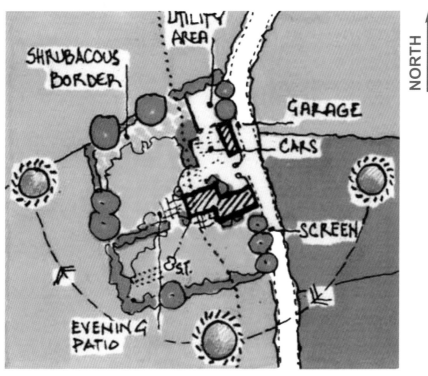

D WEST FACING SLOPE – Site Above Road

- Fall across site pushes house back up hillside with septic tank and percolation area on lower area near road
- House located towards existing northern boundary for shelter – boundary will form backdrop to house for most part when viewed from road
- Proposed garage location creates screened off car court
- New landscaping to 2 new boundaries to form native hedgerow

Conclusion: A potentially good site, but effective short-term leading to long-term privacy screening of South and West areas of house will need careful handling.

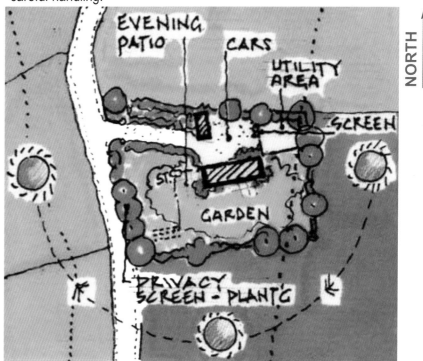

E NORTH FACING SLOPE – Site Below Road

- Fall across site places septic tank and percolation areas at lower end furthest from road
- To maximise sun and daylight the house is set back from road with its largest windows to the roadside, and the location of the outdoor sitting area to the front of the dwelling nearer the road, both of which conflict with privacy

Conclusion: This is the least favourable site as the site is north-facing and requires large windows with net curtains on elevation facing road to maximise daylight yet facilitate privacy

F NORTH FACING SLOPE – Site Above Road

- As with other sites above the road, the fall across the site requires that the house be located up hillside with the septic tank and percolation area on the lower meadow
- House located to southern edge of site because of contours
- Car court screened from road by house, garage and landscaping
- Utility area screened from house
- Southern boundary of deciduous trees to enable maximum light to dwelling in winter and summer shelter, provides backdrop to house in summer

Conclusion: Although not a great site, interesting layout enables best use of north-facing aspect.

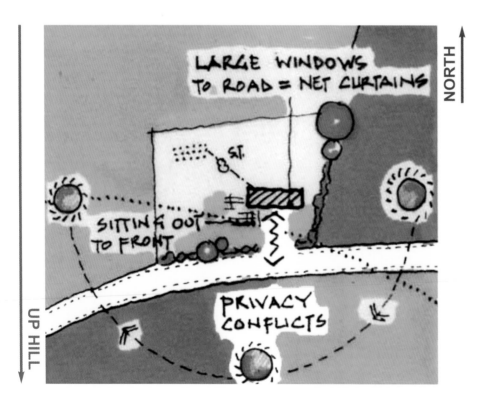

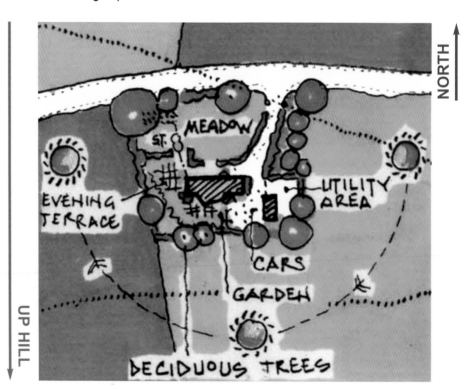

G EAST FACING SLOPE – Site Above Road

- Fall across site pushes house up hillside with septic tank and percolation area on lower meadow closer to road
- House located to northern boundary of site, off hillside access road
- Both garage and utility area located to rear of house and screened from road by garden and landscaping
- Site layout maximises privacy to evening sitting out area, however location of vehicle entrance and garage reduces size of evening patio

Conclusion: A potentially good site with safe access off a side route.

H EAST FACING SLOPE – Site Below Road

- Fall across site places septic tank and percolation area at lower area to the rear of house and away from road
- Garage location coupled with new planting screens off car court from road
- As with West Facing Site above road, boundary will form backdrop to house when viewed from road

Conclusion: Potentially a good site but effective short-term leading to long-term privacy screening of South and West areas of house will need careful handling.

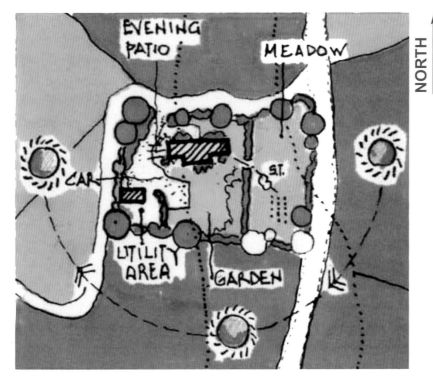

UP HILL

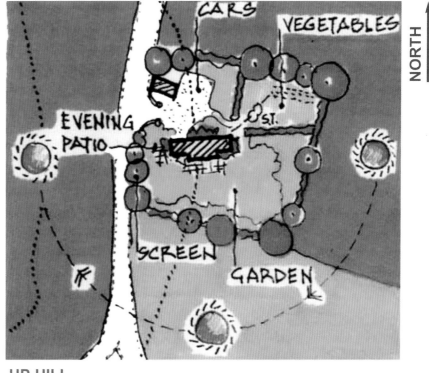

UP HILL

dealing with contours

It is important to pay particular attention to the sloping contours of the site to determine if a specifically designed dwelling could be accommodated on the site; making use of, and working with, the sloping site levels. Digging out a site, or creating an artificial platform, is expensive and can make the house unduly prominent.

In some less sensitive landscapes it may be possible, and indeed appropriate, to modify the site by excavation in order to reduce the visual impact of the development. In certain circumstances, excavation or under-building may also be used to reduce the exposure of the dwelling(s) to the prevailing winds by directing wind around or over structures while enabling a more pleasant visual integration into the surrounding landscape. However, caution should be exercised as excessive excavation can lead to permanent scarring of the landscape, in the form of a conspicuous building platform which may not be concealed by the dwelling (as per the illustration below left). Similarly excessive under-building will appear as an unnatural platform unrelated to the surrounding landscape (below right).

Where excavation techniques are adopted, the excavated material should be graded over the remainder of the site or recycled to create a landscaped garden.

Avoid over excavation. A deep gouge from the hillside creates long term land slippage problems and a poor environment for the householders

Avoid mounding up to form a flat site. This makes the house more conspicuous in the landscape, reduces its ability to retain heat/energy and exposes the exterior to the worst effects of weathering

run with the slope

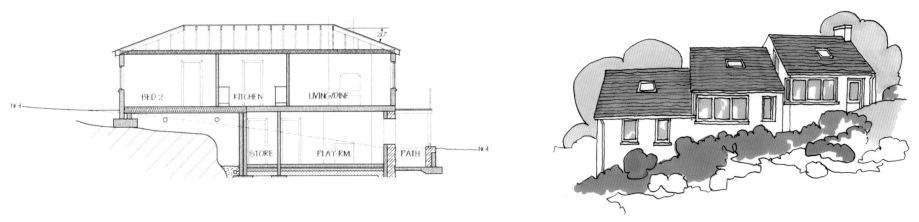

A slope can be accommodated without altering the ground, simply by changing the internal floor levels to suit. Seek a naturally flat site or cut into the hillside. Try to orientate the building with the contours to give an integrated appearance with the land, provide shelter and warmth, and reduce energy loss due to exposure.

1½ & 2 Storey Split   Contemporary Monopitch Split   Traditional Stepped Levels

rural gardens for rural houses

In part one of the guide, the importance of 'linking with the land' when choosing where to build was emphasised. The essence of this link is of course the garden and garden design which will determine how well this link is achieved. Irish country gardens stand out from their suburban counterparts by the way they embrace the house and appear to seamlessly connect to the natural landscape from which they arise. Enclosure, privacy, semi-wild habitat, the absence of expansive lawns and the appropriate rural boundary treatment are hallmarks of a more naturalistic approach.

Principles for 'natural' gardens

a planting zone between path and house softens its appearance

- Plant in tune with the landscape character of the site location;
- Avoid suburban type garden layouts and plant species - e.g. Leylandii and Grisellinia hedges, shaped dwarf Conifers, Phormiums and Pampas Grass;
- To achieve informal, relaxed garden layouts use gentle lines, curves, asymmetry etc. which appears appropriate in rural vernacular settings. Formal, symmetrical layouts with long straight lines are seldom appropriate;
- Avoid/reduce large areas of mown lawn - they are high maintenance, look 'artificial' in many rural locations and require regular application of weedkillers, which harm wildlife. Wild meadows or strimmed grass areas are lower maintenance and are frequently more appropriate;
- Create new mixed hedgerows of native/local species to maintain biodiversity and ecological regional diversity. Minimise on large single species hedges;
- Devise garden layout and select plant varieties which will attract and support wildlife;
- Select plants, or plant varieties, which are resistant to disease and 'pests' - to reduce reliance on harmful chemicals, insecticides, slug pellets, etc.;
- Limit the use of suburban 'ornamental' exotic specimen trees near roads in the countryside.

Avoid suburban layouts + garden treatment

Naturalistic planting links house to location, no visible lawn

Garden treatment without lawn between house & road

Existing & new trees settle contemporary house on site

Absence of lawn + use of backdrop anchors the house to the landscape

The rural garden - a haven for wildlife

43

creating new boundaries

Part one of the guide has indicated that sites with at least two, or preferably three, boundaries already in place, in the form of existing hedgerows or walls, should be selected when choosing a new site in the countryside. This makes completing the remaining boundaries much easier in terms of linking the house to the landscape. This can become a very difficult task if all, or a substantial amount of, the boundaries are new and are required to be put in place to give the property shelter, enclosure and privacy. Landscaping the boundaries of the house provides two useful functions: firstly, it provides shelter from the prevailing winds and secondly it can soften the visual impact of the development allowing greater integration with the surrounding countryside.

However, such is the variation of landscape character across Cork that care is needed when deciding what form new boundaries should take. In rocky uplands or coastal areas, for example, additional landscaping may not be possible or indeed desirable at all. Take your lead from the landscape character assessments in the County Development Plan and if necessary take advice from your local planning office. Otherwise take a look around and see what techniques other properties in the area have used to make appropriate boundaries and create shelter.

- Devise and develop an appropriate landscaping layout in parallel with good site layout principles - house entrance location, car area, privacy screening, creating shelter and backdrop are all integral to successful rural house design
- Commence a boundary planting programme before or simultaneously with building works
- Buffer the house as viewed from the road
- Avoid 'full frontal' - open to road site layouts

Stone walls, or stone and sod walls, as much as hedgerows, are a distinctive feature of parts of the countryside. The conservation of existing stone walls will help to root new buildings more naturally in the landscape. Traditionally Cork rural walls had a substance. All too often these are being replaced by narrow walls with busy detailing. Stone walls, or stone and sod walls, particularly in areas where they are prevalent, are preferred over plaster block work, although in some circumstances harled block work may be suitable. In general decorative brickwork or ranch style timber fencing detracts from the rural landscape and should be avoided.

Rural Roadside Boundaries and Presentation

X **Hedgerow removed** - house & site given suburban treatment

X **Hedgerow removed** - unattractive stone wall, suburban garden gives full impact of large house

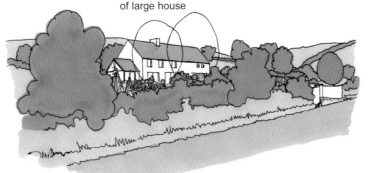

✓ **Hedgerow maintained with added planting** - house buffered from road

Wall Construction Details

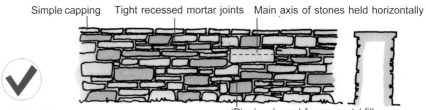

Simple capping   Tight recessed mortar joints   Main axis of stones held horizontally

'Pinnings' used for support / fill gaps

✓ **Attractive stone wall**

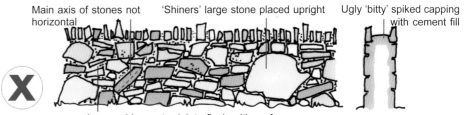

Main axis of stones not horizontal   'Shiners' large stone placed upright   Ugly 'bitty' spiked capping with cement fill

Large wide mortar joints flush with surface

X **Ugly stone wall**

✓ **Traditional attractive wall cappings**

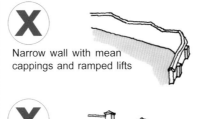

X Narrow wall with mean cappings and ramped lifts

X Mean, narrow wall, mean cappings with steps

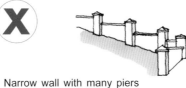

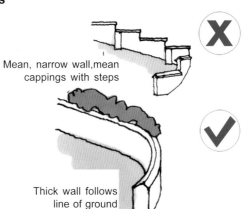

X Narrow wall with many piers

✓ Thick wall follows line of ground

Boundary walls and slopes

trees & shrubs found in cork some examples..........

- mixed hedgerow - native & introduced species
- hawthorn
- bramble
- beech (winter)
- fuschia
- blackthorn
- privet (variegated)
- gorse
- guelder rose

46

new planting

Hedgerows and shelter belts are the backbone of wildlife habitat and also help support deciduous saplings. Hedgerows are either man made or natural. Man-made hedgerows are usually at the edge of fields that have been cleared for agricultural use or have been intentionally planted for wildlife or aesthetic value. Hedgerows provide food and shelter for a variety of birds, mammals, butterflies and other insects.

When planting new boundaries (hedgerows or shelter belts) in rural areas it is a good idea to plant a variety of trees and shrubs. Planting rows of bushes or bushes mixed with a few trees is a common way to start a hedgerow. Try to choose trees and shrubs that blend with the local landscape. This is particularly important with flowering species. A selection of indigenous and naturalised hedging plants should be used. Most of these are inexpensive and easily obtainable through local garden centres. The illustrations in this section, and the annotated schedule of plant species in the Appendix, may help you with your choice.

The main factors to consider when establishing a new boundary, in order to achieve maximum benefit from the trees in terms of shelter and energy savings are:
Siting: Shelter planting should cut across the path of the wind and should be sited to make use of and improve natural shelter features, such as ridges and rocky outcrops. Planting on ridge tops is not recommended due to high levels of exposure.
Height and Length: As a rule the sheltered zone will extend for a distance of 20 times the height of the trees (e.g. if the height of the trees is 1.5m, then the area sheltered will extend for 30m) and will become effective when the length exceeds 12 times the height (e.g.if the height of the trees is 1.5 m, then shelter planting will need to cover a length of 18m to be effective).
Profile: A shelter belt should have a hedge or wind tolerant shrubs on the windward side and taller trees in the centre.
Permeability: A good shelterbelt or hedge filters the force of the wind without causing damaging turbulence.
(adapted from Building Sensitively in Ireland's Landscape)

Trees should be planted from the beginning of November until the end of March when the tree is dormant. Remember that as trees mature they require more space so should be planted, on average, at 60cm intervals. To help establish trees, choose healthy specimens under 1.5m tall.

Elm

Hawthorn (in December)

Holly and Blackthorn in flower

making an entrance

It is a common requirement of the County Council that the vehicular entrance to new developments provides clear forward visibility. The entrance must usually be recessed 4.5m from the edge of the road and have a minimum width of 3m at the inside piers, increasing to 12 m at the road edge, a minimum setback of 2.4m from the road over 50m is also usually required for visibility. Whilst this can be achieved in a variety of ways, all too often it leads to the loss of stone walls or established hedgerows located along the roadside boundary. Too often they are replaced by unsympathetic fencing, pre-cast decorative concrete blocks or crude, artificial looking stone walls.

It is the entrance gateway that presents the house to the street or road and therefore it is an important element in the overall design and layout of the dwelling and its site. Where an existing boundary feature must be removed, it can easily be replaced with an earth or sod and stone boundary, or planting of a new semi-mature hedgerow of indigenous species. Existing stone walls should be relocated behind the line of vision along the site entrance as specified by the County Council.

The layout of internal access roads from the public road to the dwelling should be carefully thought out so they can follow the contours of the site, crossing them gently in order to avoid highly visible and unnatural looking straight access roads that may be visible from long distances within the landscape. For surfacing, local gravel and tar are more natural looking and appropriate to a rural setting than tarmacadam.

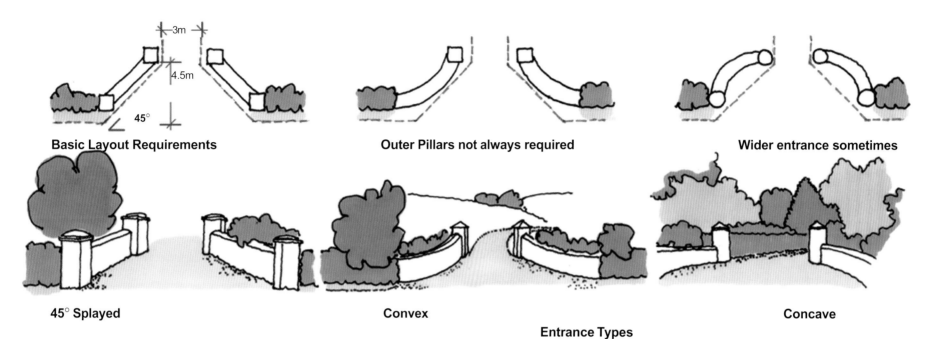

Basic Layout Requirements

3m
4.5m
45°

Outer Pillars not always required

Wider entrance sometimes

45° Splayed

Convex

Concave

Entrance Types

Gentle lines look natural - with simple stout pillars

Avoid fussy & over-elaborate entrance gates & lights
as well as spikey `frills' & `bits' on the stonework

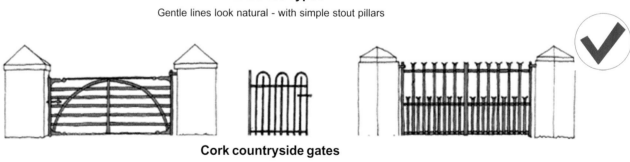

Cork countryside gates

Simple, no-nonsense, well crafted wrought iron - decent simple pillars

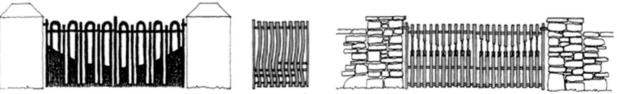

Possible contemporary metal rural gates

Informed by tradition and encourages local craftsmanship

77

summary and checklist
site layout

have you?

Fully considered the 20 items in your site selection and site layout? ☐

Achieved an orientation within 15° of south with main living spaces facing south? - i.e. have you achieved optimum aspect? ☐

Studied the options for site arrangement and addressed issues such as

   prominence? - devised a house and site layout to minimise visual impact ☐

   shelter? ☐

   privacy and screening? ☐

   presentation to the road? - attractive frontage, sufficiently buffered from the road ☐

Managed the contours of the site? - ensuring the house sits comfortably into the site ☐

Designed the landscaping and garden to link with the natural features surrounding the site? - are the new plants indigenous/native? ☐

Maintained existing roadside boundaries and supplemented with new boundary treatments appropriate to the landscape setting? ☐

Designed a discreet and safe access to the property? ☐

part three
appropriate house design

Signature characteristics of a Cork rural house

"Proportion, proportion, proportion"

Scale

Form

The problem: bigger, higher, wider

Advantages of the narrow plan form

The deep plan form

Summary & Checklist

*This guide does not address **building regulation** matters. Designers should satisfy themselves that fire safety and building regulations requirements are met. This may require specialist expertise in some cases.

78

design

As we enter this new millennium we must consider building homes which more confidently reflect our advanced technology and modern lifestyles. At the same time we have a duty to demonstrate an environmental and cultural awareness of the countryside and our built heritage. The success of truly modern rural housing in Cork will be judged on how well these two objectives are met. The aim of this guide is to promote design innovation and flair that is contemporary and firmly of its time. It is also the intention of this guide to ensure that new development acknowledges, respects and reflects the design features and characteristics that contribute to the rural character of the County.

This section of the guide has to deal with fairly complex subjects such as proportion, form, scale and massing. These subjects rarely get the attention they deserve when new houses are being planned, yet they explain why many of the pattern book houses that are built today look at odds with our design tradition in Cork and sit so uncomfortably in our landscape. The following pages are aimed at those who draw houses and submit planning applications, with the intention of reasserting some simple first principles with a view to developing more appropriate and well-mannered rural buildings. Getting issues such as proportion, scale, form and massing right and the detail can more easily fall into place. Get them wrong and no amount of frills will compensate for a potentially clumsy, awkward and unattractive structure.

It is strongly recommended by Cork County Council that, wherever possible, the services of a skilled design architect are sought to deal with these issues, particularly on sensitive or difficult sites.

Picture on opposite page - Interpretation of the simple form of the Irish cottage into a contemporary context. Incorporation of three gables produces elegant and spacious internal spaces.

contemporary rural design

81
82
83
84
85
86

88

89

90

91

92

93

94

95

96

a cork rural house ... signature characteristics

It is hoped that, by promoting understanding of the signature characteristics of our rural buildings, new rural houses will be designed that are more in harmony with our built heritage and countryside.

Signature characteristics to develop	Alien characteristics to avoid
• Simplicity of form	• Complexity of shape
• Little or no modelling of front plane of building	• Busy
• Well proportioned	• Poorly proportioned
• Balanced	• Large boxy looking
• Quality in materials	• Slap on `bits' and `frills'
• Solid, simple construction	• Proliferation of white plastic
• Absence of frills	• Suburban site treatment

Traditional buildings in Cork demonstrated basic functional scale and simple proportions and little or no decorative detailing. Simple vernacular rural dwellings were generally single storey structures, with a rectilinear plan, usually no more than one room deep, with gable end or hipped roof details. From the second half of the 19th century corrugated iron and slate replaced thatch as the dominant roofing material.

Ancillary buildings, byres and extensions were frequently added in an incremental fashion onto the gables of dwellings with lean-to roofs or split level roofs. These provided a visual break to the linear nature of the dwelling and contributed to the evolving vernacular form. Two storey dwellings were traditionally of simple classical proportions, generally retained the one room depth and had a symmetrical façade.

In summary, Irish vernacular architecture is simple, honest and has inadvertently almost effortlessly integrated into the landscape; an unconscious technique that should be mastered in contemporary rural design practice.

97   98   99   100

proportion, proportion, proportion

Architect Robert Lorimer (a much regarded designer of Scottish houses) is quoted as saying that when it came to architecture there were only three things which were important: - Proportion, Proportion and Proportion.

Certainly, proportion is fundamental to and a very significant part of successful design. It is something that affects every aspect of a house because each and every element is relative to the whole and that in turn is relative to where it is and what surrounds it.

To define or explain it is difficult. Simply put, many would say that proportion is to building what harmony is to music. To ignore or dismiss it as a design nicety is a mistake.

Traditional rural homes maintained a balance of proportions between the walls and openings (windows and doors) by demonstrating three key factors:
* height of the building relative to its openings, with openings exhibiting a vertical emphasis;
* a high solid-to-void relationship (i.e. greater wall surface area than windows and doors);
* a simple, symmetrical arrangement of features (composition);

Irish rural houses are generally characterised as being simple buildings, with horizontally proportioned roofs sitting on horizontally proportioned walls that are counterbalanced by elements with a strong vertical emphasis such as gables, chimneys and windows. This balance is destroyed all too frequently in current buildings by using much larger horizontal emphasis windows which reverse the solid-to-void relationship (i.e. the windows dominate) producing a structure that looks weak and unbalanced; lacking the simplicity and strength of traditional buildings as in the sketch above. The following pages seek to redress this

height

Current Irish building regulations advice makes it impossible to replicate the proportions of vernacular houses. Even where the openings display a vertical emphasis, the solid-to-void relationship is ruined by the larger gap between the ground and first floor windows creating a larger surface area of wall.

Building regulations and other factors have contributed to making our buildings higher, which, if insensitively handled, can overwhelm smaller scale neighbours. In order to work around this, designers of new houses will need to carefully work the section of the house to accommodate building regulations, escape windows, safe sill heights and so on, while bringing the eaves level as low as satisfactory window proportioning will allow.

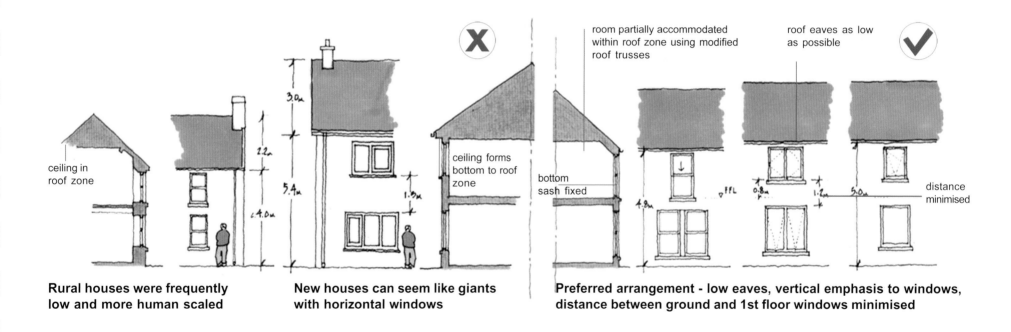

Rural houses were frequently low and more human scaled

New houses can seem like giants with horizontal windows

Preferred arrangement - low eaves, vertical emphasis to windows, distance between ground and 1st floor windows minimised

Cork County Council has made a representation to the DOE to have these amended in line with UK regulations, which permit better proportional relationships to be achieved. Using the current Irish regulations the designer should try to minimise the distance between the top of the ground floor window and the sill of the first floor window to achieve more favourable proportions.

scale

Scale is one very important aspect of proportion: the size of something relative to what is around it. It can be the size of a house relative to its site, the size of a house relative to those in the vicinity of that house, or the size of a conservatory or door relative to the type of house in which it is placed. When designing new houses in the countryside, designers need to be aware of the appropriate 'scale' of their building while at the same time still incorporating all necessary modern comforts and building regulations requirements.

- A characteristic of vernacular buildings is their human scale. The size of the door openings, eaves height and first floor ceiling height all feel more closely related to the size of the person. For many this is what gives them a great charm;
- It is more frequent today for new rural houses to be 'out of scale' with their surroundings. This is because they are bigger in terms of floor area and heights, without any measures being taken to reduce their scale;
- The scale of a new dwelling in the countryside is perhaps the key element in design consideration. It is extremely important to ensure that the building's size is relative to its surroundings. As a general rule, the larger the dwelling, the greater the impact;
- A large dwelling, regardless of single or two storey, will appear awkward within enclosed landscapes or within an area characterised by small field patterns;
- A large house needs a large site and that site needs to be set within a large scale landscape. In other words, a landscape where the views are long and there are mature landscape elements that have greater prominence than the house itself. The house should be reduced in size by being broken into smaller elements;
- It is quite simply bad manners to place a large scale new house beside an existing small dwelling, as this may result in overlooking and invasion of privacy. Be conscious of the impact your new house will have on neighbouring buildings.

A large new house out of scale (and keeping) with its neighbours
(adapted from Moray District Local Plan 1993-98: Housing in the Countryside)

Landscaping absorbs the size of the house

A large house looks completely out of proportion on a small, open site

A large house requires a large site

Satisfactorily scaled dormer with roof ✔

Poorly scaled dormer with roof ✗

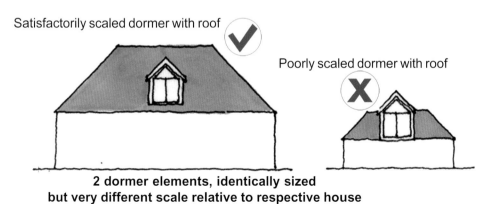

**2 dormer elements, identically sized
but very different scale relative to respective house**

Size of windows & doors make this building seem smaller - human scale

Absence of windows & large scale door make this building seem bigger

**Windows & doors also give buildings their sense of size
(both buildings in foreground are exactly the same size)**

3 Houses identically proportioned in terms of height to width etc. but very differently scaled

form
familiar building forms in the countryside

Single Storey

Cottage

'L'

'T'

Long house

'U'

'Doubled'

**characteristics
to retain**

- **Low eaves**

- **Narrow plan**

- **35°-55° roof pitch**

- **Modest scale**

- **Vertical emphasis
 to gables**

- **Sturdy and solid**

- **Natural finishes**

- **Flat fronted**

- **Well-mannered**

1 + Half Storey

No dormer

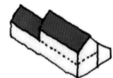
Single eaves dormer

Twin eaves dormer

Triple eaves dormer

Small roof dormer

Unusual dormer

Two Storey

Simple 2 storey

Long 2 storey and lean-to

Long 2 storey and 'T'

2 storey and 'L'

Combined Long

Doubled and slipped

Hipped

Single storey

Simple 2 storey

2 storey and 'L'

2 storey and 'U'

2 storey and 'T'

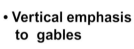
Thatched

Other Miscellaneous Forms

Tower

Tower with block

Tin hayshed

Tin Haysheds doubled

Tin roof lean-to

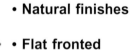
Tin and slate roof lean-to

pattern book forms, alien to the countryside

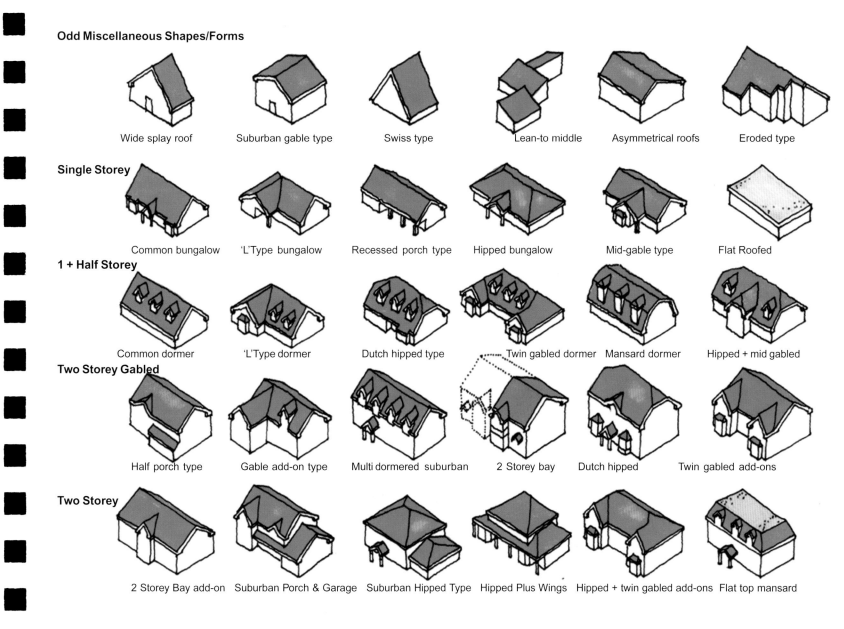

Odd Miscellaneous Shapes/Forms

Wide splay roof   Suburban gable type   Swiss type   Lean-to middle   Asymmetrical roofs   Eroded type

Single Storey

Common bungalow   'L'Type bungalow   Recessed porch type   Hipped bungalow   Mid-gable type   Flat Roofed

1 + Half Storey

Common dormer   'L'Type dormer   Dutch hipped type   Twin gabled dormer   Mansard dormer   Hipped + mid gabled

Two Storey Gabled

Half porch type   Gable add-on type   Multi dormered suburban   2 Storey bay   Dutch hipped   Twin gabled add-ons

Two Storey

2 Storey Bay add-on   Suburban Porch & Garage   Suburban Hipped Type   Hipped Plus Wings   Hipped + twin gabled add-ons   Flat top mansard

characteristics to avoid

- **Highly modelled**
- **High eaves**
- **Wide gables**
- **Low or no roof pitch**
- **Bulky and squat**
- **Awkward scale**
- **Synthetic finishes**
- **Plastic clad**
- **Decorative frontage**
- **Many additional details**

the problem: bigger, higher, wider

the problem with house sizes today

Cork cottage: Simple form, narrow widths, steep roofs, vertically proportioned windows, central chimney at gable, natural local finishes.

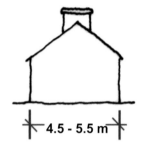

Typical Cottage - Linear Plan organisation

4.5 - 5.5 m

The 70's bungalow: Wide plan - dark central corridor, shallow pitched roof, horizontally proportioned openings, imported synthetic finishes.

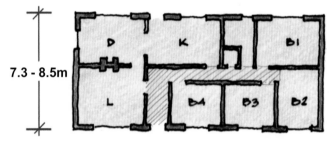

7.3 - 8.5m

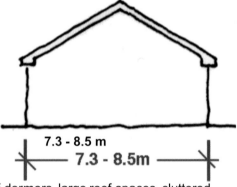

Typical Bungalow- Double room depth internal corridor

7.3 - 8.5 m
7.3 - 8.5m

The 90's 'big house' - Double deep plan, bulky proportion, off centre chimney, shallow roof pitch, adorned frontages, mid-roof dormers, large roof spaces, cluttered finishes.

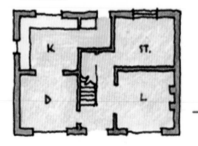

gives →

or →

or →

Current Composition
Double room depth plan

Unsatisfactory 1$\frac{1}{2}$ Storey

Suburban 2 Storey Type

Unsatisfactory "Traditional" Copy

one solution - break down the bulk, get the massing right

Modern pattern book houses differ radically in form to those more familiar buildings of the countryside. It is an issue of bulk, size and scale - big houses, wide gables, deep plan forms, squat and `overweight'. Massing is about how you assemble the elements of the house - in one big bulky overweight mass, or in an assembly of more slimmed down elements. Solutions lie in breaking down massing using `traditional' better proportioned forms.

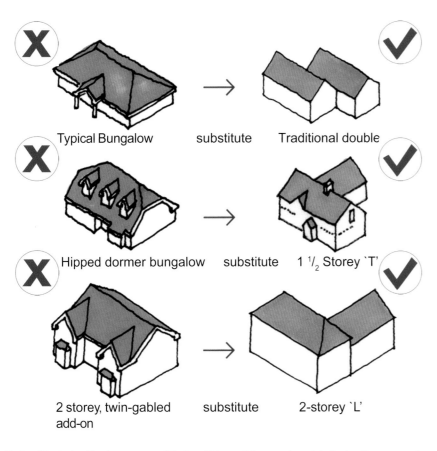

Typical Bungalow   substitute   Traditional double

Hipped dormer bungalow   substitute   1 ½ Storey `T'

2 storey, twin-gabled add-on   substitute   2-storey `L'

Substitute bulky houses with traditional forms to obtain better massing

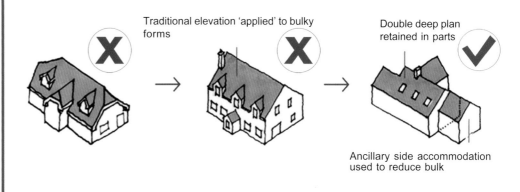

Traditional elevation 'applied' to bulky forms

Double deep plan retained in parts

Ancillary side accommodation used to reduce bulk

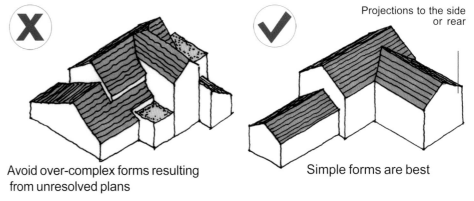

Avoid over-complex forms resulting from unresolved plans

Projections to the side or rear

Simple forms are best

Guidance also seeks to avoid poor substitution

the narrow plan form ... some advantages of ...

Parallel to slope - Large platform cut

90° to slope - Large platform cut

DOUBLE ROOM DEEP PLAN - Inflexible on slopes

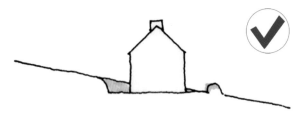

NARROW PLAN - Parallel with slope - narrow depth reduces cut

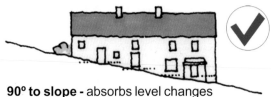

90° to slope - absorbs level changes

1 Building on a slope is easier

Internal corridor receives no natural light.

Some main living spaces receive little sunlight.

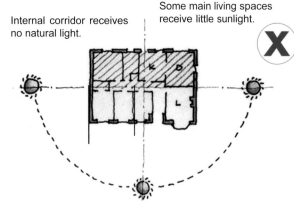

DOUBLE ROOM DEEP PLAN -
50% of house does not benefit from solar gain

Small windows/ openings on shady (north) side

Narrow buffer zone to north incorporating utility areas, porch stairs etc...

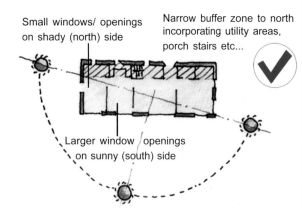

Larger window openings on sunny (south) side

NARROW PLAN - Preference for house to face south east, if possible, to maximise on heat gains in winter & reduce over heating problems in summer.

2. Heating costs can be reduced by 30%

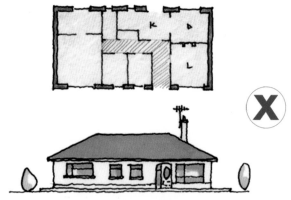

DOUBLE ROOM DEEP PLAN - typical plan layout with internal corridor places constraints which dictate the size and location of windows resulting in too much glass in relation to masonry.

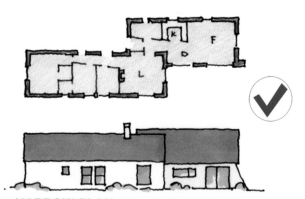

NARROW PLAN - plan facilitates window glazing options. Leads to more satisfactory ratio of glass to masonry. Greater freedom in composition.

3. Breaking away from double deep plan allows better balance of glass to masonry

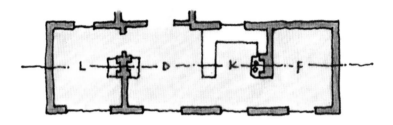

Contemporary open plan within traditional form

Contemporary house with traditional form. The narrow plan house avoids the need for excessively tall, or shallow pitched roofs.

Extensions and additions should be directed to the gable end or rear elevation

The narrow plan form reduces the need for an excavated platform
The house elements are broken down and follow the contours

Spatial Diversity - Departing from the double deep plan facilitates spatial interest. These dynamic and contemporary interiors are based on the narrow plan form.

the deep plan form in a rural context

As seen earlier, the double room depth plan is the format used for most new rural houses today, due to efficiency in maximising rooms under one large roof. The consequence of this however, is that new single and two storey houses tend to be at odds with our Cork vernacular. Here we examine reworking a typical double deep house, whilst still maintaining a similar number of rooms, area and other efficiencies. On this page a 12.2m (40') x 9m (30') plan footprint is maintained, while a better proportioned houses is achieved by using traditional gable dimensions with lean-to roof and other modifications.

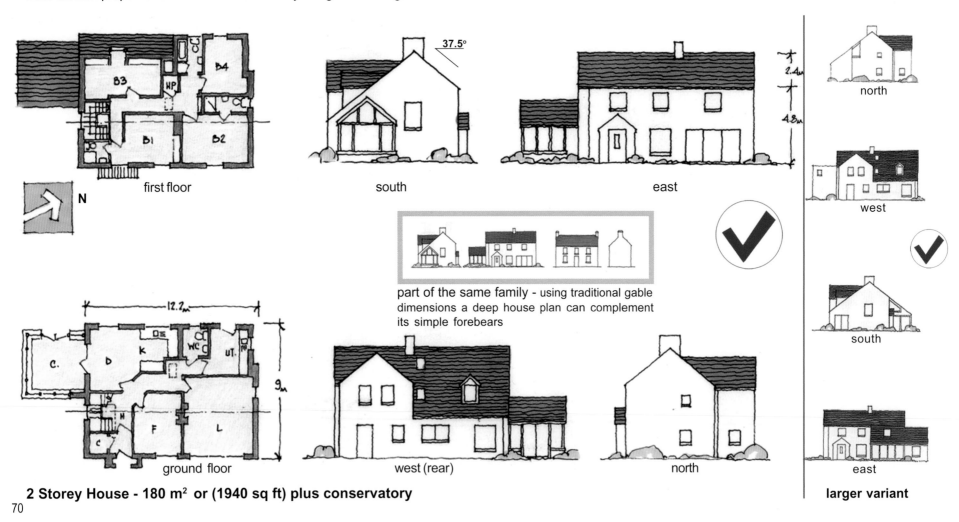

first floor

south

east

north

west

part of the same family - using traditional gable dimensions a deep house plan can complement its simple forebears

south

ground floor

west (rear)

north

east

2 Storey House - 180 m² or (1940 sq ft) plus conservatory

larger variant

alternative traditional types

The problem presented by the double room deep plan house type within the Cork countryside is essentially one of form and scale. The typical roof form generated by this plan type is an overly dominant feature of such houses. Combinations of hipped roofs and deep overhanging eaves exacerbate the problem and result in over sized and out of scale roofs. These examples show that elegantly simple rural house designs can accommodate the double room depth footprint (12.2m x9m, or 40' x30'), yet remain faithful to Cork's heritage. These will sit better in the countryside than most patternbook designs. As with the example on the facing page, this example uses traditional gable dimensions with a rear lean-to roof. Whilst not advocating that all new houses should be traditional, this illustration serves to demonstrate that good proportioning is possible for larger houses. A more contemporary and innovative interpretation of the deep plan form is explored in Appendix One by Mary Kerrigan Frank Harkin Architects.

If well detailed, these types would be more suitable than most pattern book models for those who do not wish to employ a designer.

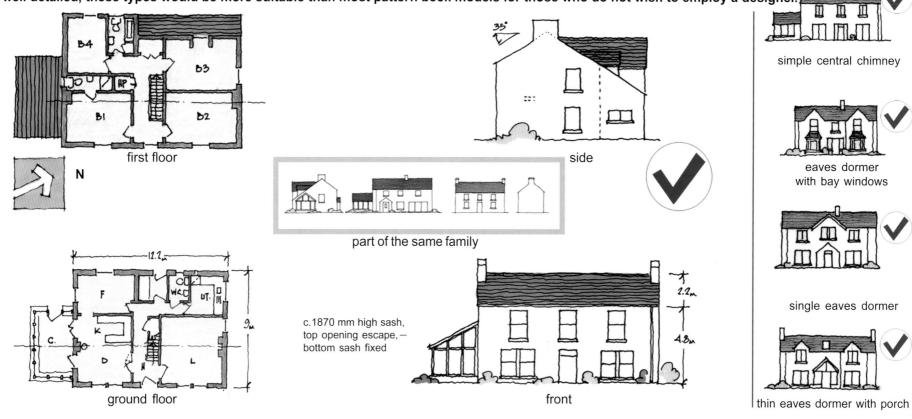

first floor

N

side

part of the same family

ground floor

c.1870 mm high sash, top opening escape, bottom sash fixed

front

simple central chimney

eaves dormer with bay windows

single eaves dormer

thin eaves dormer with porch

2 Storey House - 186 m² or (2000 sq ft) plus conservatory

variants of the same plan

105

106

107

108

109

110

111

112

113

summary & checklist
design

have you:

Developed a house that is simple in its form - is the form related to rural building forms of Cork? ☐

Designed a house that incorporates distinctive characteristics of its location within rural Cork? ☐

Achieved attractive proportions in the building design? ☐

Developed a plan which will allow a good solid-to-void relationship in its windows and doors? ☐

Ensured the house is in scale relative to:

its site - does the choice of single or two-storey respond to the character of the site? ☐

surrounding buildings - is the scale appropriate to the existing character of the locality? ☐

Broken down the massing of the house to articulate different elements in order to reduce its bulk where necessary? ☐

Opposite page: Castlepark, Kinsale - a superb study of form, scale, proportion and detail. A notable feature of Castlepark is the way in which the architect achieved a very high solid-to-void relationship (i.e. large areas of masonry) whilst at the same time managing to incorporate large glazed openings carefully balanced by use of rooflights.

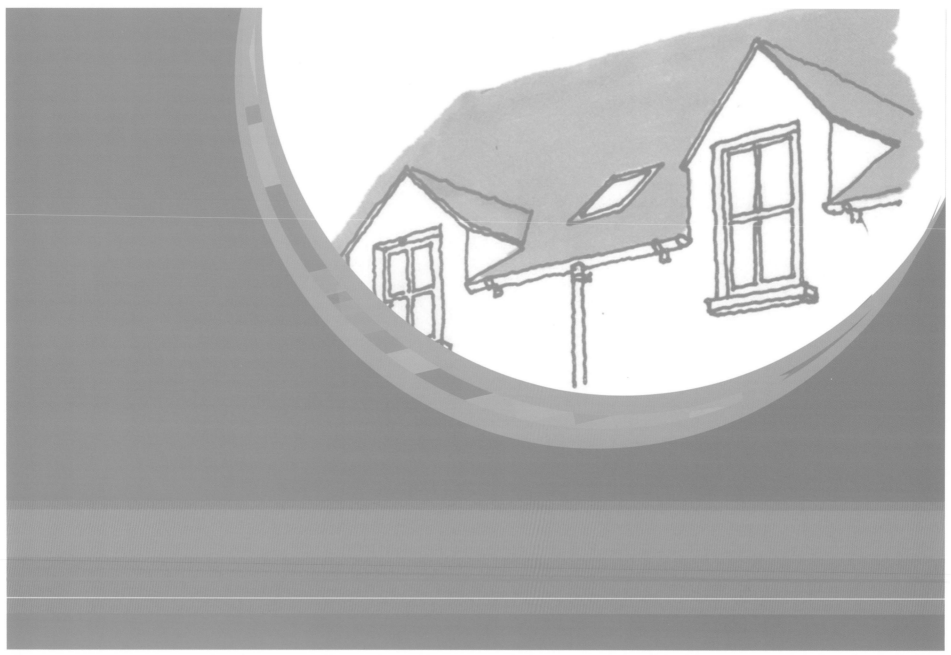

part four
good construction

Elements:

- Roofs
- Chimneys
- Windows
- Dormers and Rooflights
- Doors
- Porches and Canopies
- Conservatories and Sunspaces
- External finishes
- Stone
- Colour
- Summary & Checklist

*This guide does **not** address **building regulation** matters. Designers should satisfy themselves that fire safety and building regulations requirements are met. This may require specialist expertise in some cases.

114

good construction

This section is devoted to design detail and construction to focus attention on a range of critical design elements frequently overlooked but which are fundamental to the successful appearance of our new rural homes. These elements are only relevant once the issues of proportion, scale, massing and form have been successfully tackled. The section deals with issues that appear straightforward but are often mishandled, poorly constructed or result in clumsy and ugly detailing.

Opposite page: rough cast render applied to surface of building can have a striking effect and protect the structure from the elements.

roofs - slate, tiles, metal sheeting, thatch, glass, zinc

A roof lends a building its distinctive profile. Roofs of Cork rural houses tend to be simple shapes: hipped or gabled, and generally sloped 35° - 55°. Other shapes are of course possible, but only where they are conceived with skill and will be executed with care. The interesting and colourful roofs of Cork rural buildings contribute to the striking architectural characteristics of many local areas. The material used for roofing is an important aspect of local architecture, both functionally and aesthetically.

- Blue grey slate, thatch and painted corrugated sheeting are traditional rural Cork roofing materials;
- The way the roof edges are constructed is critical to the successful appearance of a house. Today almost 100% of new houses are constructed where the roof sits as a 'lid' oversailing the external walls. More often than not these are finished in white PVC, a detail that, perhaps more than any other, sets them part from our rural vernacular context. Traditional rural roof edge details that are low maintenance can be easily achieved today, using painted plaster or dark coloured PVC. This gives new houses a more immediate direct connection with neighbouring buildings and maintains regional identity - something which Cork County Council is anxious to actively encourage;
- With the exception of the occasional Victorian house or ornate gate lodge, the edges of Cork rural house roofs tended to be very simply treated. For this reason scalloped or ornate fascias are generally to be avoided;
- Care is also required with thick format roof tiles; these are more suited to large simple roofs only. Small format roofing tiles/slates are the best material for smaller roofs, such as bay windows, dormers, porches, etc.;
- Simple black round plastic rainwater goods are recommended. These have the advantage of attractive lines reminiscent of cast iron, are very economic and do not easily show grime and dirt over time. White plastic or square section rainwater goods, on the other hand, have few of these features and should generally be avoided. They also require regular maintenance, which they rarely receive, to avoid becoming grimy in appearance;
- Higher statutory insulation standards for dwellings will mean thicker roof construction build up. Great diligence and skill will be required by designers and house builders to reconcile heat loss issues with attractive detailing.

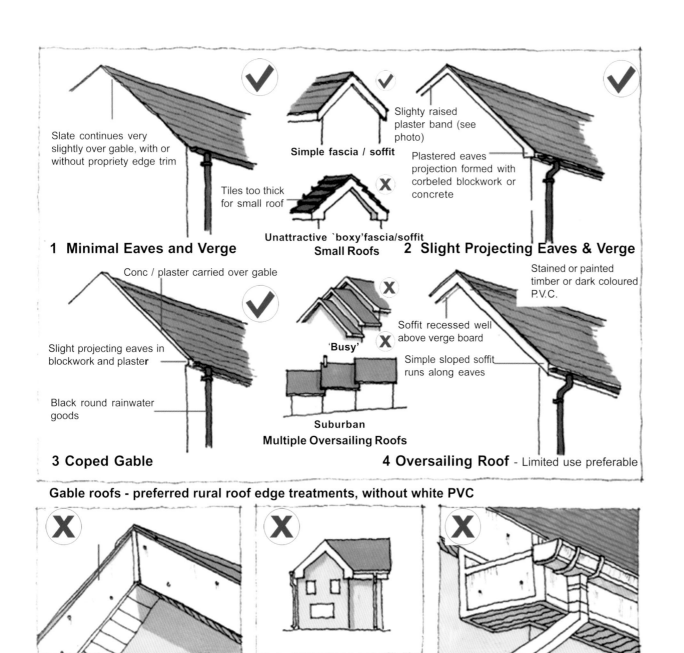

Slate continues very slightly over gable, with or without propriety edge trim

Tiles too thick for small roof

Simple fascia / soffit

Slighty raised plaster band (see photo)

Plastered eaves projection formed with corbeled blockwork or concrete

Unattractive `boxy'fascia/soffit
Small Roofs

1 Minimal Eaves and Verge

2 Slight Projecting Eaves & Verge

Conc / plaster carried over gable

Slight projecting eaves in blockwork and plaster

Black round rainwater goods

'Busy'

Soffit recessed well above verge board

Simple sloped soffit runs along eaves

Stained or painted timber or dark coloured P.V.C.

**Suburban
Multiple Oversailing Roofs**

3 Coped Gable

4 Oversailing Roof - Limited use preferable

Gable roofs - preferred rural roof edge treatments, without white PVC

Avoid box verges

Avoid heavy lid

Avoid box eaves

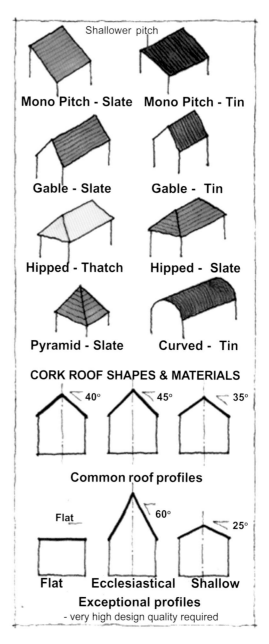

Shallower pitch

Mono Pitch - Slate   Mono Pitch - Tin

Gable - Slate   Gable - Tin

Hipped - Thatch   Hipped - Slate

Pyramid - Slate   Curved - Tin

CORK ROOF SHAPES & MATERIALS

40°   45°   35°

Common roof profiles

Flat   60°   25°

Flat   Ecclesiastical   Shallow

Exceptional profiles
- very high design quality required

79

chimneys

Chimneys are a very important element of a house, much overlooked today. They have the potential to add substance and presence to the appearance of a house. Poorly positioned, meanly built, or a total absence of, chimneys can detract enormously from a house.

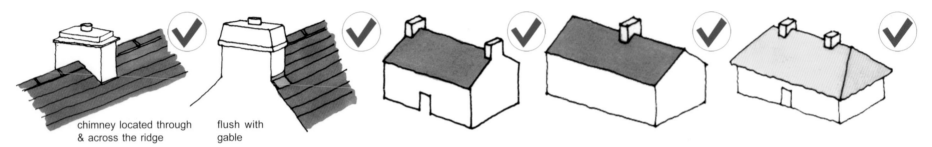

chimney located through
& across the ridge

flush with
gable

Chimney stacks add interest to a house and as a general principle for rural houses they should be located through and across the ridge. Where chimneys are located at gables, they should preferably be flush with the face of the wall, as is a feature characteristic across most of Cork. In East Cork, however, stout stacks built proud of the gable are a feature typical to the area.

Care and attention is required with the detail and construction of chimneys and cappings. Rural chimneys tended to be strong elements, whereas today they can often appear narrow and weak. The requirement today for passive flue vents to internal bathrooms and toilets and below slab radon sumps gives reasons for chimneys to incorporate several flues. Capping details vary across the county, giving local identity. Whilst thin ("mean") chimneys are to be avoided, heavy or clumsy detailing of chimney cappings can be equally unsightly if care is not exercised.

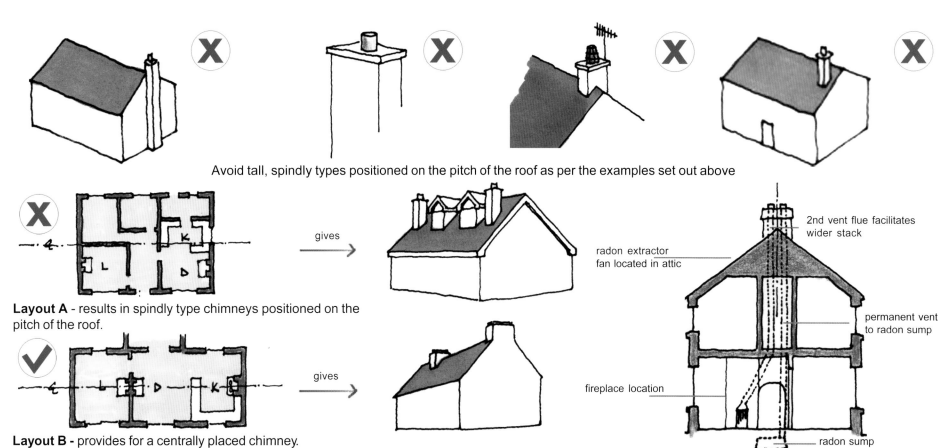

Avoid tall, spindly types positioned on the pitch of the roof as per the examples set out above

Layout A - results in spindly type chimneys positioned on the pitch of the roof.

gives →

Layout B - provides for a centrally placed chimney.

gives →

2nd vent flue facilitates wider stack

radon extractor fan located in attic

permanent vent to radon sump

fireplace location

radon sump

The plan layout of a house affects the position of chimneys

Offset fireplace remedy

windows <small>size, shape and arrangement of openings</small>

All houses require natural light and therefore need openings. Being the predominant openings of a building, the size, shape and positioning of windows significantly influences the scale and proportions of the dwelling. Windows are perhaps the most difficult aspect of houses to get right. In the past, size and shape was limited by construction materials and costs, which meant that window openings tended to be small and away from corners. Consequently openings were surrounded by large areas of solid wall creating what is known as a high `solid to void' relationship, giving a strong and sturdy appearance to our rural buildings. Today there is no such constraint. Current practice is to use an increasing selection of larger, wider windows with a variety of shapes, often with unfortunate consequences and which tend to look at odds within the much simpler rural setting.

Naturally brightly lit interiors are desirable and for any room to be adequately lit, the area of glass should not be less than 10% of the floor area. It is worth noting that highly glazed façades are possible in certain locations provided they are conceived with skill and executed with care, using attractive framing materials.

assymmetry not uncommon

too many windows

too low solid-to-void

swiss cheese effect

large openings are possible

Simple guidance on window openings might be summarised as follows:

- Keep the range of opening sizes to a minimum and the shape of openings simple. Arrange openings in order to maximise a high solid-to-void appearance where it matters - i.e. work the plan to limit the number of openings in some places, using rooflights and concentrating large openings to the main living areas which ideally will have the most sun and view, remembering that highly glazed façades are often best located where they are not fully in public view;
- Keep the arrangement of openings simple, observing the central axis generated by the shape of the wall. This axis is particularly strong and demands more attention where pitched roof shapes are used, such as with gable ends or dormers;
- Vertical emphasis of openings is generally preferable to horizontal emphasis;
- Windows should be centred either exactly on the axis, or purposefully off the axis. Openings slightly or equally off the axis are very discordant in appearance. Dormers, rooflights and first floor windows are traditionally centred over ground floor windows. As a general principle these should not be bigger than the lower level windows.

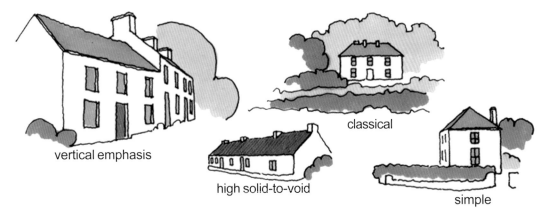

vertical emphasis

classical

high solid-to-void

simple

Cork Rural Context

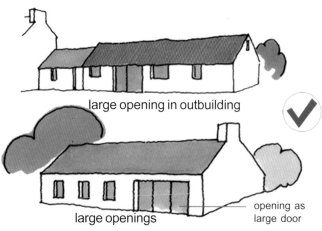

large opening in outbuilding ✓

large openings

opening as large door

Balancing Large Openings

typical bungalow - horizontal windows ✗

rotate openings 90°

higher solid-to-void effect ✓

Vertical Openings Appear Appropriate

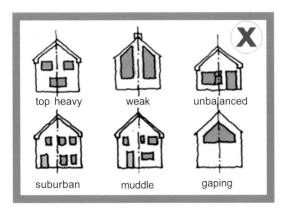

✗

top heavy

weak

unbalanced

suburban

muddle

gaping

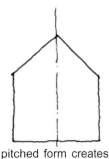
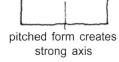

pitched form creates strong axis

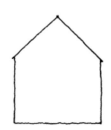

no openings - strongest

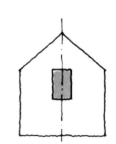

centred - not too large

✓

deliberate off-centre

Openings in Gables

windows proportion, division and materials

Windows are one of the most important features of a building; the choice of window style affects the visual personality of a house. Depth of profile, elegance and proportion in windows needs to be considered as windows can weaken the elevation if set too close together, or too close to the corner. Today, windows frequently receive little of the care and attention to proportion and construction they were assigned in the past. Well made, attractive windows can hugely enrich a building. Similarly poor window design, or cheap-looking window construction, often spoils the appearance of an otherwise satisfactorily designed new home. Window design should maintain proportion and simplicity.

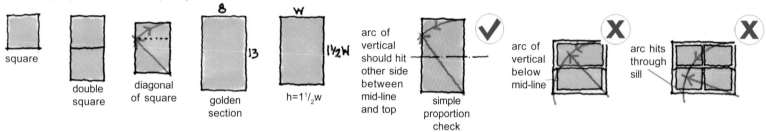

square

double square

diagonal of square

golden section

h=1½w

arc of vertical should hit other side between mid-line and top

simple proportion check

arc of vertical below mid-line

arc hits through sill

Proportion and Vertical Emphasis: Simple Rules of Thumb

Windows do not have to be small to respect tradition. Larger windows can offer spectacular views, but the length to width ratio needs to be considered. In many cases, a series of smaller windows with vertical emphasis, or of square proportion, sit more comfortably than large horizontal openings. A number of methods can be employed to integrate larger windows into rural buildings as depicted below.

horizontal openings need care

divide into vertical openings

drop sill and divide

change window to door opening

bay window

Ways to Incorporate Horizontal Openings in a Rural Context

136

137

138

139

    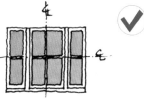

| Equal about vertical axis | Equal about horizontal axis | Fixed opening light used to balance opening light | Top hung opening | Side hung opening slender sections | Tilt and turn opening | Traditional sashes to wide opening |

Good window division

Good window division is generally based on two principles, the first is to divide the window exactly symmetrically about the central horizontal or vertical axis or sometimes both. The second is to use a window type or system which facilitates division giving glass panes of identical size (or as near as) e.g. vertical sliding sash or similiar.

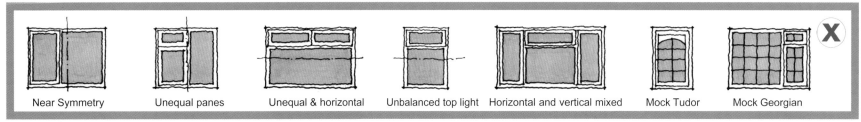

| Near Symmetry | Unequal panes | Unequal & horizontal | Unbalanced top light | Horizontal and vertical mixed | Mock Tudor | Mock Georgian |

Window division to avoid

Windows should be made out of the best quality materials affordable, both in terms of appearance and performance. Traditionally windows were made of painted timber which has several advantages including freshness of colour, slenderness of sections and depth of profile. Timber joinery craftmanship is still strong in Cork. Alternatively many firms offer timber window systems which can be factory finished, stained or aluminium clad minimising maintenance. Otherwise windows in metal and plastic are available in a greater range of colour finishes. Some plastic window systems can appear very chunky and two dimensional, especially where false Georgian bar strips are used - something which should be especially avoided. Higher glazing thermal performance requirements demand even greater vigilance with respect to many of the above points.

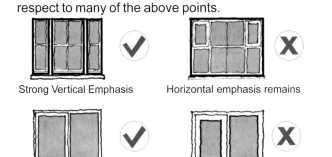

Strong Vertical Emphasis   Horizontal emphasis remains

Fenestration highlighted

Nearly the same size   Squinting

Fenestration less obvious

Window construction fundamental to design
good and poor realisation

Colour: white highlights division

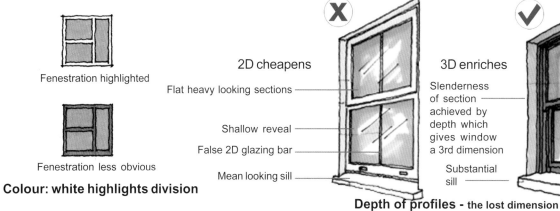

2D cheapens   3D enriches

Flat heavy looking sections

Shallow reveal

False 2D glazing bar

Mean looking sill

Slenderness of section achieved by depth which gives window a 3rd dimension

Substantial sill

Depth of profiles - the lost dimension

dormers and rooflights

Changes in building construction techniques along with the extensive use of the double deep plan have helped to give rise, over the past 20 years, to the dormer bungalow house. On previous pages we have highlighted some of the disadvantages of this house type. Those together with the fact that dormers are so often finished in white PVC cladding can make them bulky and prominent in terms of the overall appearance of the house. That is not to say that there is no place for the dormer house. As illustrated within Part 3, modifications can be made to reduce the bulk of houses accommodating ancillary wings or eaves dormers. However, in many instances, depending on the site context and potential layout, a full two storey buiding may be preferable to a proliferation of dormers and rooflights. In general, dormers should only be incorporated in rural house design with restraint and care, following a few basic principles as set out below:

- 'Busy' eaves lines or roof planes should be minimised;
- The unseen slopes of roofs allow more scope for the inclusion of multiple or larger dormers, where absolutely necessary;
- In most instances rooflights are preferable to mid-roof dormers, especially on the visible public slopes of roofs;
- A full two-storey house may, depending on location, be preferable to the use of dormers.
- If dormers are used, simple wall-plate dormers (traditional eaves dormers) are the preferred form. Again care is required to how they are constructed and detailed;
- Avoid the use of white PVC side cladding, box fascias and soffits to dormers - stained timber or slate offer far more attractive alternatives;
- The location and frequency of rainwater downpipes (RWPs) needs to be considered from the outset with eaves and dormers. A proliferation of rainwater downpipes, especially white, on the front of houses should be avoided;
- Flashings which allow rooflights to sit flush with a slate roof finish are widely available, and their more extensive use is actively encouraged by Cork County Council.

140   141   142   143

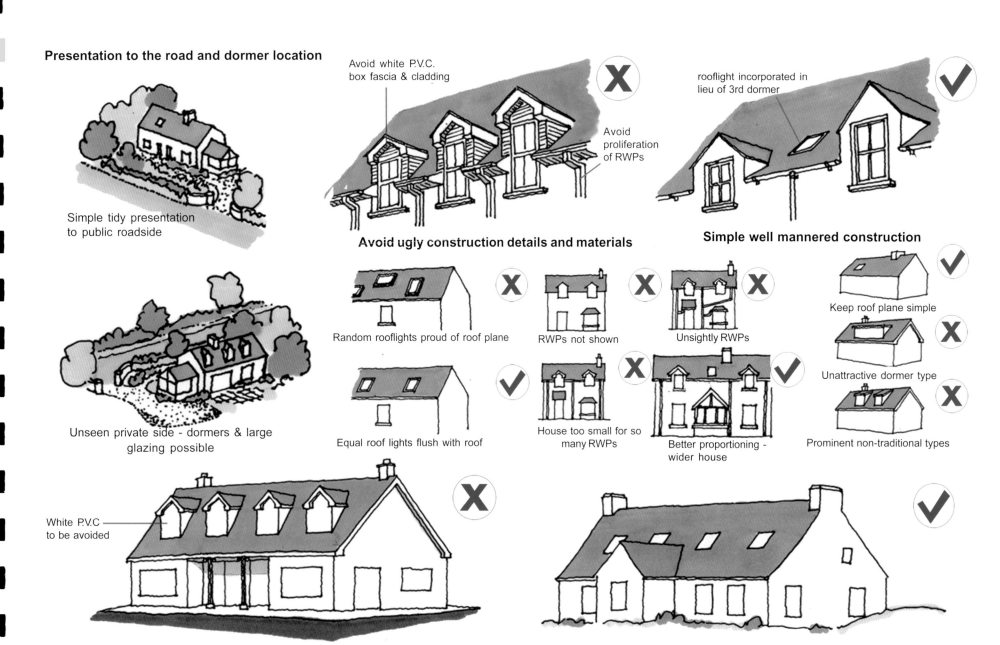

Presentation to the road and dormer location

Simple tidy presentation to public roadside

Unseen private side - dormers & large glazing possible

Avoid white P.V.C. box fascia & cladding

Avoid proliferation of RWPs

Avoid ugly construction details and materials

rooflight incorporated in lieu of 3rd dormer

Simple well mannered construction

Random rooflights proud of roof plane

RWPs not shown

Unsightly RWPs

Keep roof plane simple

Equal roof lights flush with roof

House too small for so many RWPs

Better proportioning - wider house

Unattractive dormer type

Prominent non-traditional types

White P.V.C to be avoided

Avoid prominent mid-roof dormers

Preferred rooflight option keeps roof plane simple

87

doors

Traditionally much care was taken with this element of the house. Frequently it was the only item of embellishment on the otherwise simple exterior of Irish country, town and city buildings. Proportion, colour and detail are fundamental to making external doors an attractive feature of a house, as per the basic principles below:

- Doors should always reflect the shape of the opening and are most successful in their simplest form - in sheeted or panelled timber;
- Front doors should be viewed as an opportunity to introduce interest, contrast and enrichment to a house;
- White PVC, aluminium or varnished tropical hardwood reproduction doors are actively discouraged and should be avoided. Sustainable painted or natural hardwood alternatives are becoming more readily available for external joinery and their use is actively encouraged by Cork County Council;
- With conservation or refurbishment work, skilled joiners can replicate the detailing and features of period doors accurately;
- Discretion in the selection and use of colour in Cork countryside houses has traditionally been used to great effect to enhance design. Strong contrast in colours between, say, a boldly painted front door and plainer surrounding walls can bring significant visual interest and style. New exterior wood coating products are available for finishing timbers which are a good substitute for high gloss paints, offering a more `maintenance friendly' finish;
- Whilst the door and surround often needs to admit light to the hallway, large glazed panels in doors can look over-elaborate. A window above or beside the door, as in the traditional examples, is a good compromise, which leaves the simple door intact. Fanlights over doors can also be used to increase light to hallways;
- Carefully consider electrical lighting to the front door. Avoid bulkhead type light fittings and explore other light fittings and options for location;
- Avoid unsightly, prominent location of ESB meter boxes. These can easily be discreetly located (refer to illustrations on facing page).

144 145 146 147

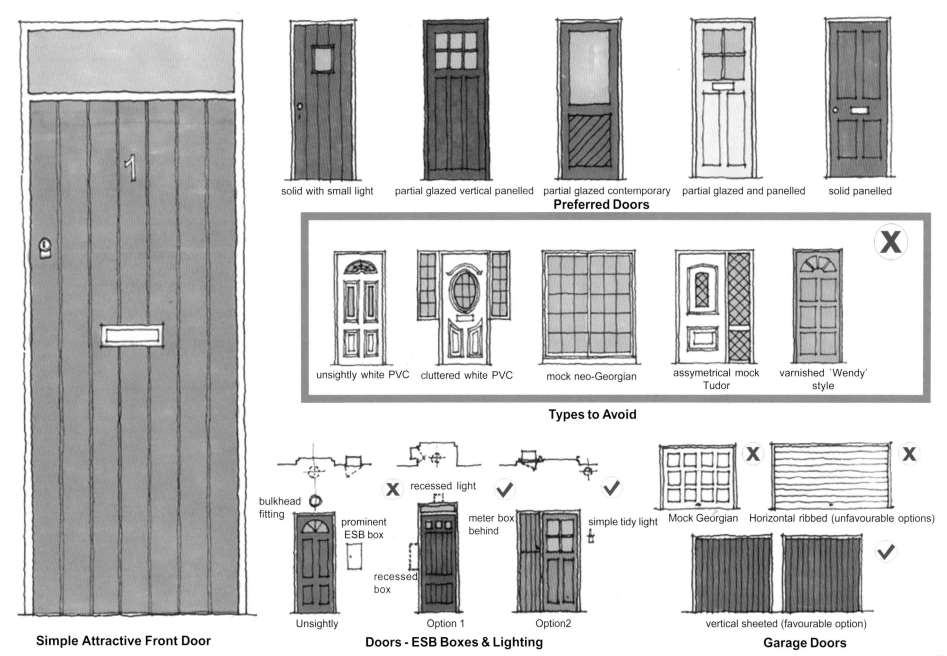

Simple Attractive Front Door

solid with small light | partial glazed vertical panelled | partial glazed contemporary | partial glazed and panelled | solid panelled

Preferred Doors

unsightly white PVC | cluttered white PVC | mock neo-Georgian | assymetrical mock Tudor | varnished `Wendy' style

Types to Avoid

bulkhead fitting | recessed light | meter box behind | simple tidy light

prominent ESB box

recessed box

Unsightly | Option 1 | Option2

Doors - ESB Boxes & Lighting

Mock Georgian | Horizontal ribbed (unfavourable options)

vertical sheeted (favourable option)

Garage Doors

porches and canopies

A key characteristic of Cork rural houses is that there is little or no modelling of the front plane of the building. Porches expressed on the outside of houses, or add-on canopies were much rarer than today. Occasionally small porches or canopies were found over older cottage doors, particularly on single storey houses. These add interest to the building, however it was rare to find porches on 2-storey houses as the cost combined with the very low sill level of the first floor windows of the typical 3-bay rural farmhouse made their inclusion very difficult. Today, the need to compensate for the difficult proportioning arising from regulation heights, together with the increased size of our homes gives rise to virtually every new house having an expressed porch or canopy to the front of the house, which is generating very busy lines in our countryside.

Furthermore, good sustainable energy efficient design practice demands the inclusion of buffer zones in our houses between the inside and outside to reduce heat losses as people enter and leave. Many older houses have such buffer zones internalised within the house, leaving the outside unadorned; a practice we should emulate today.

In summary we need to ask the question do porches need to be placed at the front of the house? Cork County Council would encourage the placement of porches to the side, rear, or better still internalised within the volume of the house.

Where porches are incorporated, the following points should be considered:
*   Porches should be carefully detailed and built with good quality materials - avoid white plastic where possible;
*   The size and shape of the porch should be well proportioned. Small roofs do not need rainwater goods;
*   Introducing a different material for this element only, such as brick or stone, should not be necessary on simple houses;
*   The use of `mock' or `false' classical type porches are best avoided.

148   149   150   151   152

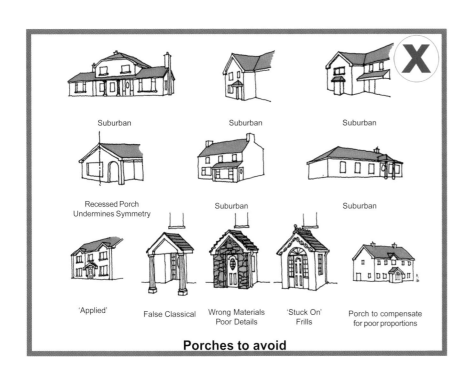

Suburban

Suburban

Suburban

Recessed Porch
Undermines Symmetry

Suburban

Suburban

'Applied'

False Classical

Wrong Materials
Poor Details

'Stuck On'
Frills

Porch to compensate
for poor proportions

Porches to avoid

Simple Canopy

Traditional Canopy

Simple shelter to front door

Simple porch form + detail

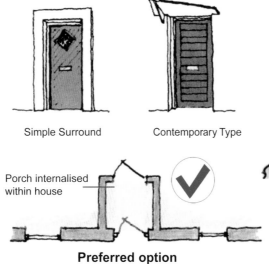

Simple Surround

Contemporary Type

Porch internalised
within house

Preferred option

Contemporary alternative

conservatories/sunspaces

Conservatories or sunspaces can be very attractive features of new houses or, more commonly, subsequent additions to older houses. They can act as very useful visual `release-points' in more solid houses. Many new eco-houses are designed with the sunspace as the central organising element (in terms of orientation, plan arrangement and section) to maximise passive solar heating gains and bring down energy costs to a fraction of that of normal houses. These eco-houses require very careful siting. Reconciling technical and aesthetic requirements can be quite difficult and demands great skill.

- The shape of the sunspace should be consistent with the house to which it is attached.
- The size and location of an ancillary type sunspace requires careful consideration with respect to proportion, size and the spatial layout of the house. Sunspaces immediately beside kitchens will be most extensively used;
- Avoid conservatories/sunspaces, which are 'out of scale' with the rest of the house;
- The construction materials of the sunspace are fundamental to its successful appearance. 'Flat' white PVC profiles are generally the least successful due to their bulky sections and garishness of their particular white colour. Many firms offer low maintenance roofing framework in attractively profiled sections, along with timber framework to the sidewalls;
- Revised building regulations seek to minimise heat losses from these elements of houses. This impacts on the design of all new sunspaces in terms of extent of glazing and framework, with doors to seal off from the rest of the house. This aspect of sunspace design will require much more careful consideration in the future;
- First floor conservatories are particularly difficult, both in terms of their visual appearance/obtrusiveness and possible privacy issues. Generally they should be avoided. If they are used, a much more skilled approach is required;
- It is preferable that glare and over-heating concerns are dealt with either by reducing the extent of glazing, or the use of blinds, rather then using heavily tinted glass;
- Ventilation is fundamental to successful sunspace design in terms of comfort. The location and disposition of opening windows/vents impacts significantly on the overall appearance and needs to be considered from the outset.

153   154   155   156

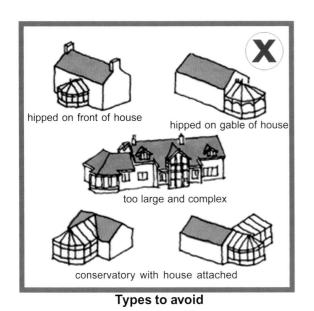

hipped on front of house

hipped on gable of house

too large and complex

conservatory with house attached

Types to avoid

simple lean-to

`A' pitch to gable

`A' pitch to rear. Careful proportioning if to front

lean-to to rear careful material selection if to front

simple hip shape can look well

Preferred Shapes and Locations

controllable blinds

controllable ventillation opening

Winter Day

Maximise on passive solar

Minimise visibility to public roads unless very well proportioned & executed

Dark metal or stained painted timber finish

Large Glazed Lean-to

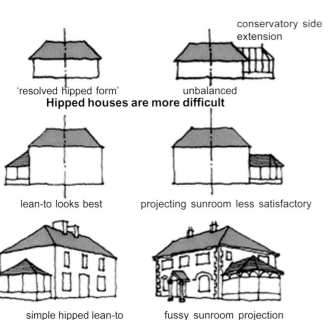

conservatory side extension

'resolved hipped form'

unbalanced

Hipped houses are more difficult

lean-to looks best

projecting sunroom less satisfactory

simple hipped lean-to

Rural Solution

fussy sunroom projection

Suburban Approach

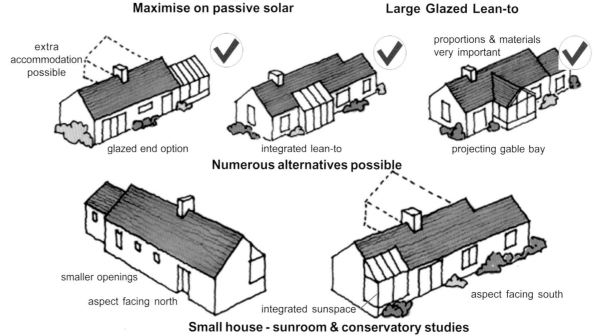

extra accommodation possible

glazed end option

integrated lean-to

proportions & materials very important

projecting gable bay

Numerous alternatives possible

smaller openings

aspect facing north

integrated sunspace

aspect facing south

Small house - sunroom & conservatory studies

external finishes ... regional characteristics

Not only does the particular shape of a building give a region its identity, but also the finishes applied, or as importantly not applied, to the outside of a building show distinct regional variations. For example, as one travels across Cork, the coastal fishing villages of the west are very distinctive with their brightly coloured painted houses. Kinsale, on the other hand, is particularly noted for its slate hanging to external walls. This was a practical measure arising as a means to prevent the continuous driving rain penetrating internally. Interestingly this is also a feature of coastal villages of the southwest of England with which Kinsale historically has strong links. Further east and north, thatch as a roofing material is far more commonplace.

East Cork is notably high in limestone, which gives a very different appearance to the stone walls of the countryside in the east, being built of stones that are roundish and light grey in colour. Perhaps for this and associated reasons, colours, as one heads north and east across the county, become more muted - typically limewash greys, off whites and soft yellow ochres.

Brickworks were located around Youghal and elsewhere in the east of the county, where clay, suitable for making brick, was found and consequently brick houses are more common. Elsewhere in Cork brick was often used for practical reasons to construct parts of the walls, forming corners and arches, such as around door and window openings, external corners and chimney stacks. More often these elements were then plastered over to give the building a uniform appearance and resist water penetration. The recent trend of hacking off the render finish to the outside of buildings has exposed these brick elements. This is regrettable as many building interiors are now at risk from water penetration, while also the uniformity and clarity of our vernacular is becoming confused. New houses are being built to replicate the stripped houses, which were never meant to be seen, producing houses with stone cladding or non-functional brick applied around corners, to chimneys and so on. Similarly brick and stone or concrete should not be mixed randomly 'for effect' or as 'features'.

Upgrading of the traditional style to suit our modern lifestyle can lead to proliferation of pipe work and cabling associated with modern appliances, which can disrupt architectural features or elevations. Locate pipework internally wherever possible and consider painting pipes to blend with the roofs or walls of principal elevations so as to minimise their visual impact.

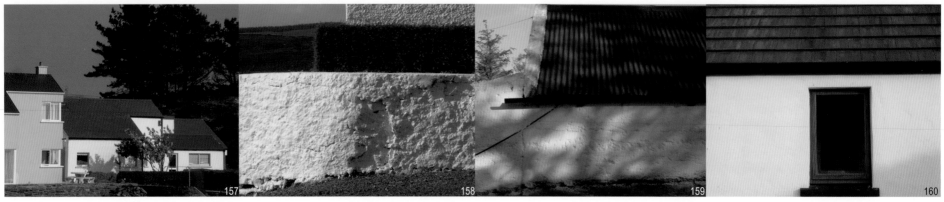

157   158   159   160

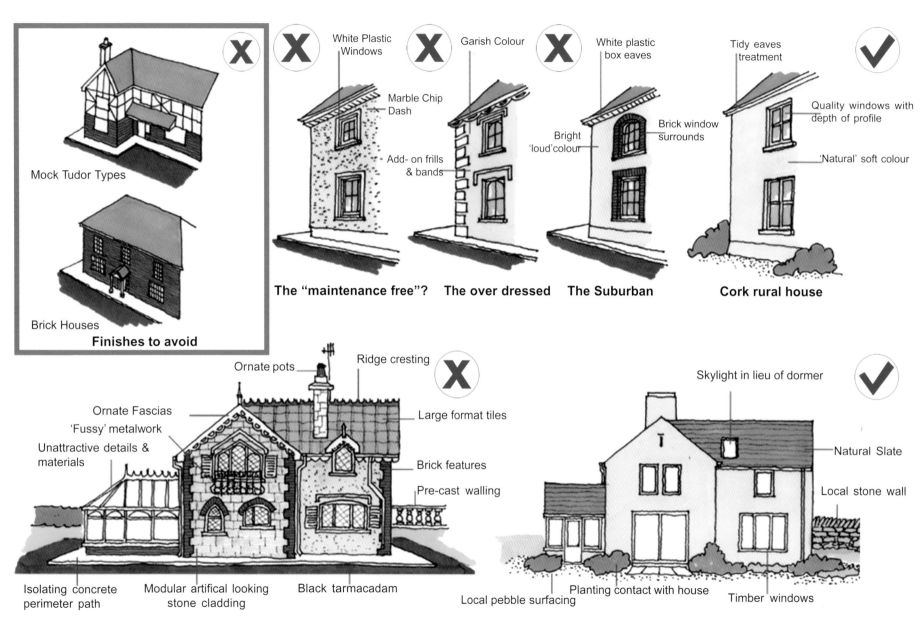

Finishes to avoid

Mock Tudor Types

Brick Houses

The "maintenance free"?

- White Plastic Windows
- Marble Chip Dash
- Add-on frills & bands

The over dressed

- Garish Colour

The Suburban

- White plastic box eaves
- Brick window surrounds
- Bright 'loud' colour

Cork rural house

- Tidy eaves treatment
- Quality windows with depth of profile
- 'Natural' soft colour

Expensive add-ons & frills used to compensate for poor design

- Ornate pots
- Ridge cresting
- Ornate Fascias
- 'Fussy' metalwork
- Unattractive details & materials
- Large format tiles
- Brick features
- Pre-cast walling
- Isolating concrete perimeter path
- Modular artifical looking stone cladding
- Black tarmacadam

Contemporary rural house continues tradition of simplicity

- Skylight in lieu of dormer
- Natural Slate
- Local stone wall
- Planting contact with house
- Local pebble surfacing
- Timber windows

stone

It is important to be aware that while traditional Cork rural houses were, more often than not, built with stone or clay walls, they almost always had painted plaster finish – a characteristic which should be retained and continued by and large. The render finish applied to the walls was necessary to act as an `overcoat' to the houses, keeping the water out, given the severe driving rain across the County. Rough cast renders were the traditional external coatings applied to rubble-walled buildings. Materials such as marble chip finish and some pebble dashes, which are intended to be maintenance free, not only frequently appear at odds with the locality but also deteriorate and grow unsightly over time, and should generally be avoided.

Stone finished buildings do exist, but these tended to be either 'grand' cut stone structures such as churches, banks, and courthouses, or utilitarian structures such as outbuildings, barns, mills and so on. This created an attractive clarity in the hierarchy of rural buildings types while at the same time forming a uniformity to the appearance of our houses in the region.

Notwithstanding the above, stone used with consideration and skill can be very attractive, and such use is to be encouraged as follows:

- Stone cladding to ancillary 'wings' or other elements such as garden or boundary walls can provide attractive contrast and help reduce the apparent size of buildings;
- Certain landscapes or sensitive locations can benefit substantially where stone is used extensively on the outside of a house to marry it harmoniously with the site;
- Stone can also be used very successfully in more skilful contemporary houses, providing an interesting play of heavy and light materials;
- An important but general rule where stone is to be employed is that, where possible, it should be of the locality so that there is a consistency in colour that links successfully with other stone structures, ditches, rock outcrops, etc. in the immediate vicinity. For example, a light grey limestone boundary wall typical to East Cork would look very incongruous among the blue slate/shale of Baltimore and vice versa;
- Avoid 2-dimensional type effects with stone, which give it a very false 'applied' appearance. Traditional Cork rural buildings have an honesty and simplicity – values which are worth retaining and emulating in new rural buildings.

161

stone finishes

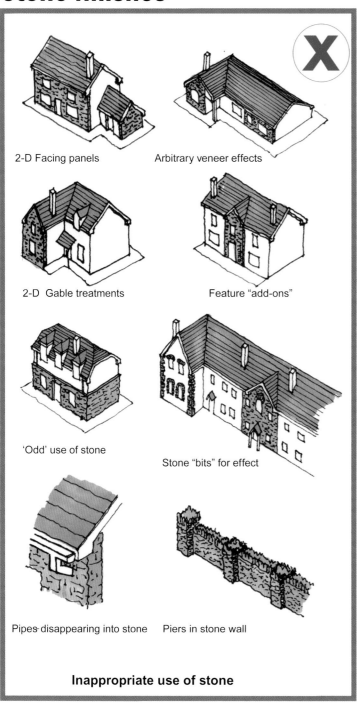

2-D Facing panels

Arbitrary veneer effects

2-D Gable treatments

Feature "add-ons"

'Odd' use of stone

Stone "bits" for effect

Pipes disappearing into stone

Piers in stone wall

Inappropriate use of stone

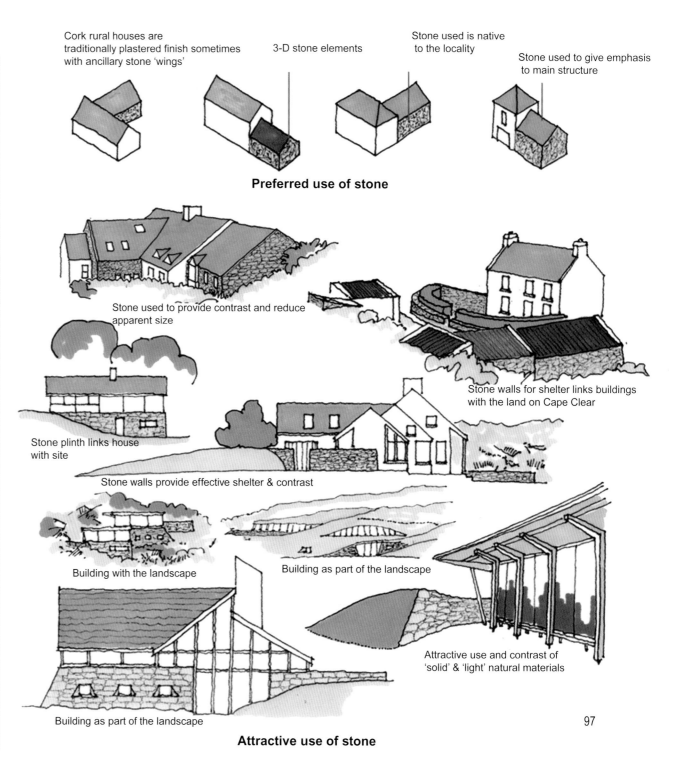

Cork rural houses are traditionally plastered finish sometimes with ancillary stone 'wings'

3-D stone elements

Stone used is native to the locality

Stone used to give emphasis to main structure

Preferred use of stone

Stone used to provide contrast and reduce apparent size

Stone walls for shelter links buildings with the land on Cape Clear

Stone plinth links house with site

Stone walls provide effective shelter & contrast

Building with the landscape

Building as part of the landscape

Attractive use and contrast of 'solid' & 'light' natural materials

Building as part of the landscape

Attractive use of stone

colour

The choice of colour and materials makes all the difference to the impact of a house on the rural landscape. The most important principle is to use colours which blend in with local traditions and surrounding buildings. In general, the use of earth colours on buildings in the countryside will best complement the natural environment through the seasons and reduce impact, particularly given the larger size of today's homes.

Historically, whitewash was the decorative material used in domestic architecture. A light grey or ochre colour was also used. In some parts of the county, notably West Cork, the enthusiastic use of colour was one of the dominant features of local architecture. In North Cork the use of colour is much more restrained, with a more prevalent use of off whites and greys.

Simple guidance for colour selection is to prepare a colour chart of the main hues of vegetation to appear on a site and its immediate surroundings, including the seasonal variations throughout the year, and use this as an aid to the most appropriate choices.

A key characteristic of rural vernacular building is that the use of strong contrast between the differing finishes of roofs, walls, and doors is frequently the sole means of introducing visual interest or giving a `lift' to such buildings. It is this discretion in the use of colour that greatly enhances such simple design.

As a general principle, light colours should be used on walls complemented by strong colour, particularly on the door. Roofs tend to reflect more light than the walls, therefore dark colours are more desirable. Dark colours on roofs, such as the blue/grey of natural slate, reduce the apparent size of buildings, whereas light or reflective materials increase apparent size, drawing attention to them. The colour should match that of neighbouring buildings. Painted corrugated tin roofs complement white walls. The use of strong colours, the reds, greens and browns of the iron roofs of rural buildings create a distinctive image for rural architecture.

163   164   165   166

167

summary & checklist
constuction details

have you:

Considered the roof profile, i.e. height and pitch of the roof, to blend in with the local environment? ☐

Used roofing materials that respect and reflect the tradition of their location and surroundings? ☐

Detailed roof edges that are appropriate to their context? ☐

Carefully located the chimney positions and ensured there is substance to their appearance? ☐

Arranged the openings, i.e. doors and windows, to provide good natural light and views whilst maintaining an attractive composition overall? ☐

Used good quality windows and doors that are attractive in terms of size, design and materials, and are responsive to local traditions? ☐

Used windows and doors that comply with fire safety regulations; energy conservation regulations; and disabled access regulations? ☐

Where dormers or rooflights are used, ensured that they are carefully detailed to minimise visual impact? ☐

Where a porch is to be included, questioned whether it must be expressed or can it be internalised? ☐

Where a sunspace is incorporated, designed it so that it respects the proportions and materials of the house and is energy efficient? ☐

Used materials and finishes in a way that is consistent with the local character, enriching the house's appearance? ☐

Used colour effectively to enhance the building whilst still appearing satisfactory within the landscape? ☐

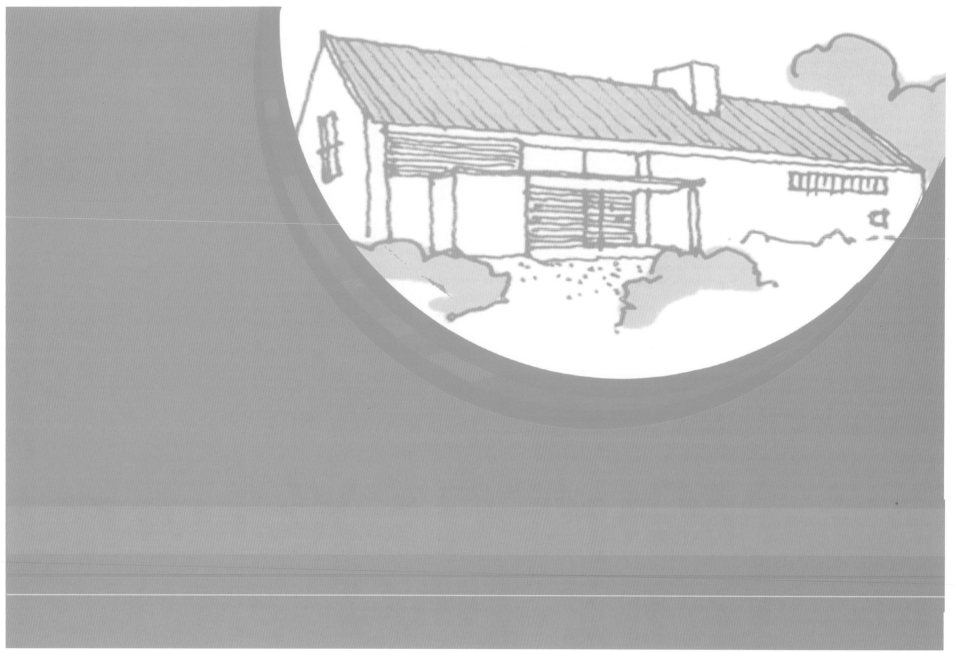

part five
worked example

- **Pre-planning preparation: site analysis and sketches**
- **Planning Application Contents**
  - **Cover Letter for planning application**
  - **Site Notices (including map showing location of site notice)**
  - **Planning Application Form**
  - **Site Suitability Assesment Report**
  - **Planning Drawings (detailed sketches)**

worked example

Low eaves, Simple form, Larger glazed area to south, Simple detailing, Slate roof, Strong chimney, Limited palette of quality materials

bringing it all together

Using the advice set out in the previous sections, this section shows how all the various considerations may be pieced together to produce the most favourable outcome for the site in question. This is a step-by-step example of all the details that should be included in a planning application to enable the planner to swiftly assess your application for a house in the Cork countryside. The first three pages show illustrations used in analysing the site and developing the design, while the following pages show the information required for a planning application for the scheme

For this worked example a north-facing site has been selected, and the layout and house design in this case is a very contemporary one, but draws upon elements of Cork tradition to ensure that the finished development blends well into the locality. An unusual design such as this may require specialist input to demonstrate compliance with building regulations but this would not affect the planning application itself.

It is worth noting that local OS Discovery series maps, which are readily available in most newsagents, can be very useful in assessing a site's prominence.

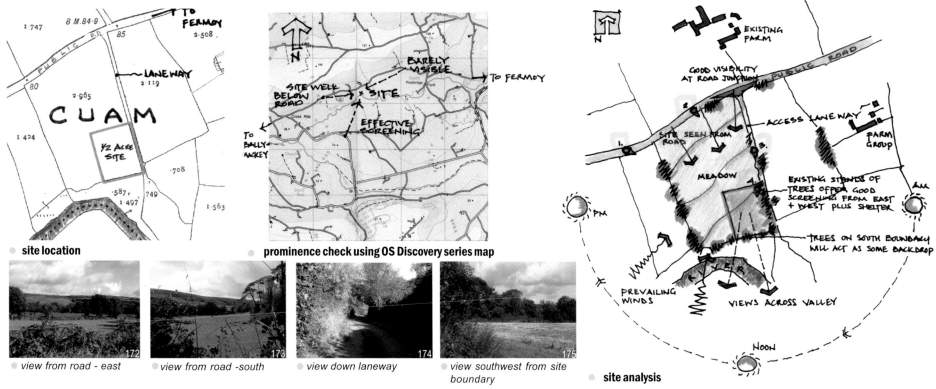

- site location

- prominence check using OS Discovery series map

- view from road - east

- view from road -south

- view down laneway

- view southwest from site boundary

- site analysis

(pre-planning preparation)

preplanning

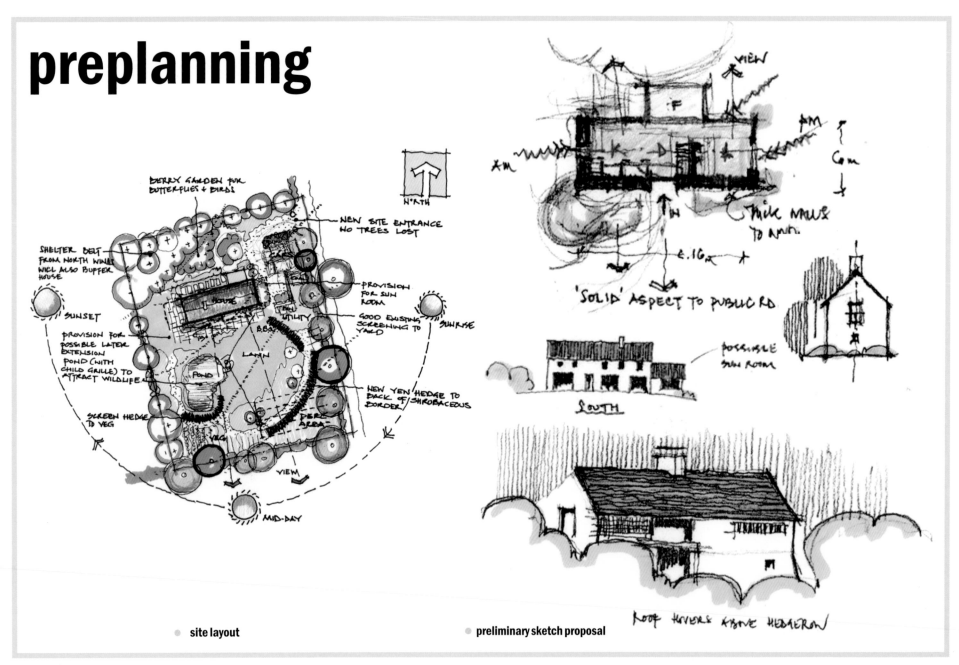

site layout

Labels on site layout:
- BERRY GARDEN FOR BUTTERFLIES & BIRDS
- NEW SITE ENTRANCE NO TREES LOST
- SHELTER BELT FROM NORTH WINDS WILL ALSO BUFFER HOUSE
- PROVISION FOR SUN ROOM
- GOOD EXISTING SCREENING TO YARD
- SUNSET
- PROVISION FOR POSSIBLE LATER EXTENSION POND (WITH CHILD GRILLE) TO ATTRACT WILDLIFE
- SUNRISE
- SCREEN HEDGE TO VEG
- NEW YEW HEDGE TO BACK OF/SHRUBACEOUS BORDER
- MID-DAY
- VIEW
- NORTH
- HOUSE, UTILITY, BBQ, LAWN, POND, VEG, PERG AREA

preliminary sketch proposal

Labels on sketch proposal:
- VIEW
- F, K, D
- AM
- COM
- THICK WALLS TO NORTH
- E.16x
- 'SOLID' ASPECT TO PUBLIC RD
- SOUTH
- POSSIBLE SUN ROOM
- ROOF HOVERS ABOVE HEDGEROW

sketch design of narrow plan house

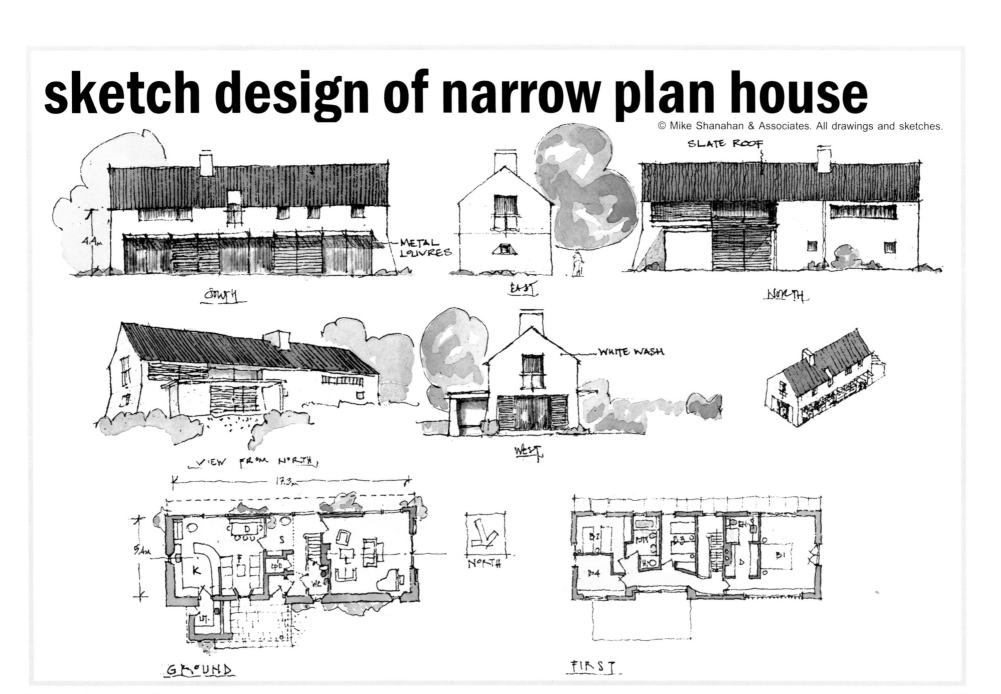

SLATE ROOF

METAL LOUVRES

SOUTH

EAST

NORTH

WHITE WASH

VIEW FROM NORTH

WEST

NORTH

GROUND

FIRST

cover letter

C. ANDRAUGH AND PARTNERS . ARCHITECTS

No 1 T E E S Q U A R E S O U T H . F E R M O Y . Co C O R K
t 0 2 2 5 5 5 5 5 5 . f 0 2 2 5 5 5 5 5 6 . e can@draw.net

Planning Department,
Cork County Council,
Model Business Park,
Model Farm Road,
CORK.

8th November 2002

Dear Sirs,

RE: PERMISSION TO CONSTRUCT NEW HOUSE AND INSTALL SEPTIC TANK
AT CUAM, BALLYMACKEY, FERMOY FOR SEAN AND MARY MORIARTY

In connection with the above Planning Application we enclose the following documentation;

- 6 Copies of the completed Application Form
- 2 Copies of Press Notice, which appeared in the Irish Examiner on 7th November 2002.
- 2 Copies of Site Notice, a copy of which was erected on Site on 8th November 2002.
- 6 Copies of drawings comprising;

2002/P/01	Site Location Plan at scale 1:2,500
/02	Site Layout Plan at 1:250
/03	Ground Floor Plan/Elevations at 1:100
/04	First Floor Plan/Elevations/Section at 1:100

- 6 Copies of Site Suitability Assessment Report including Test hole layout plan
- Planning Fee Cheque in the sum of Euro 65.00

We trust the above is satisfactory and look forward to your favourable decision.

Yours faithfully,

Andrew Pencil.

Andrew Pencil, Architect
C. ANDRAUGH AND PARTNERS

Encls.

notices

CORK COUNTY COUNCIL
SITE NOTICE

I/We, **SEAN & MARY MORIARTY** [2], intend to apply for

Permission ☑

Outline Permission ☐

Permission for Retention ☐

Permission consequent on the grant of outline permission ☐
(Ref. No. of outline permission; _____)[3]

For development of this site at

CUAM, BALLYMACKEY, FERMOY
_____[4]

The development will consist/consists[5] of

CONSTRUCT 2 STOREY HOUSE
AND INSTALL SEPTIC TANK
_____[6]

The planning application may be inspected at the offices of the Planning Authority, Model Business Park, Model Farm Rd, Cork, during normal opening hours, i.e. 9.00a.m. to 1.00p.m. and 2.00 p.m. to 4.00 p.m. Monday to Friday (excluding public holidays).
A submission or observation in relation to the application may be made in writing to the planning authority within the period of 5 weeks beginning on the date of receipt by the authority of the application, on payment of a fee of €20.

Signed: *M Moriarty* [7]

Date of erection of site notice **8/11/2002**

See directions for completing this notice attached to this form.

Strong all-in v

STRONG winds from with some heavy squalls, fleet for the opening ra GlaxoSmithKline all-in winter s the Royal Cork.

Two boats were particularly outs the decent sized entry. Donal D-Tox won in the Echo handica second in IRC while Derr Genevieve was winner in IRC ar Echo. However, there is a long ro with racing over the coming five Sundays leading to the final event on December 8, competition is certain to be hot.

Officer of the day

St. Aengus', Mountrath v Kilkenny City V.S. off tomorrow: St. Finian's C.C. v Fingal C.C. OFF; C.C.C. 2-6 O'Carolan Col., Nobber 0-3; Bush P.P. Oldcastle OFF TILL FRI; Ballymahon Sec. Sch.; V.S. 1-2; Ardsc. Ph., Granard 2-20 Oaklands Co. North Leinster Schools SF C; Killina Pres, Sec. Kilbeggan OFF

Carrick on Suir V.S. 2-8
Colaiste Troase Kanturk 0-8
TWO first half goals helped Carrick on Suir V.SF over Colaiste Treasa Kanturk in the Munster Se Vocational Schools Senior hurling at Ballygibby.
SCORERS: Carrick on Suir V.S.: B Butler 1-4 (fr. 1-1, P Diffley 0-2(0-1 free) D McGrath 0-1,...
Colaiste Treasa: W Murphy, 0-2 frees; K Holan McCarthy 0-2; J Guinee 0-1; A Barry 0-1 free.
CARRICK ON SUIR: J Murphy, P Cronin, S P Norris, M Cronin, N Kenny, A Walsh, R McGra Gates, S Butler, P Diffley, D Reid, K Reid, T Cro Hogan for T Cronin.
COLAISTE TREASA: B Mullane, D O'Riorda M Kearney, P O'Riordan, A Barry, J Duggan, K Guinee, K Holland, W Murphy, D McCarthy, D O'Connor, M O'Riordan, Subs T O'Keeffe for Murphy for E O'Connor
Referee: D Cahill (Ballygorean)

HOCKEY
Intervarsities 2nd day's play in Dangan, C
Men: NUIG 0 Trinity 2 (A Cuppage, D Johnso Ulster 10 (R McCandless 7, J Quigley 2, I Mor Queen's 1 Univ. of Limerick 0: UCD 0 UCC 0; R Willis, C Wilson, D Clonnemond) Univ. of Lin (D Rene 3) Trinity 0; RCS I 0 NUIG 2 (M Cann Univ. of Ulster 1 (A Ferguson) DCU 0.
Women: Univ. of Limerick w.o. v DC U, UCD Limerick 1 (L Kane); UCC 6 (S D'Leary, V Fen Carey, C Kennefick, A English, J Lawson 2) C 2 (B Walsh, P Keenan) Trinity 3 (C Rowan, A Trinity 10 (K Wallace 3, D Joyce 3, A Flinn 3, 2 UCD 3 (R Keegan, C Sullivan, S Walker) G 2 (B Walsh, P Keenan) Univ. of Ulster 5 (L Alcorn 2, J A Leeburn, S Herron) R CSI 1 U Kerin).
Today's fixtures: Men (Mauritius Cup Ser UCD: UCC v Univ. of Ulster.
Women: (Chilean Cup) Semi-finals - U C C v N U I G: Univ. of Limerick v Trinity. Finals at Women 3.0; Men
4.30.

PITCH AND PUTT
BRINNY: Fourball last Sunday, winners, ne

Rural PLACE Map

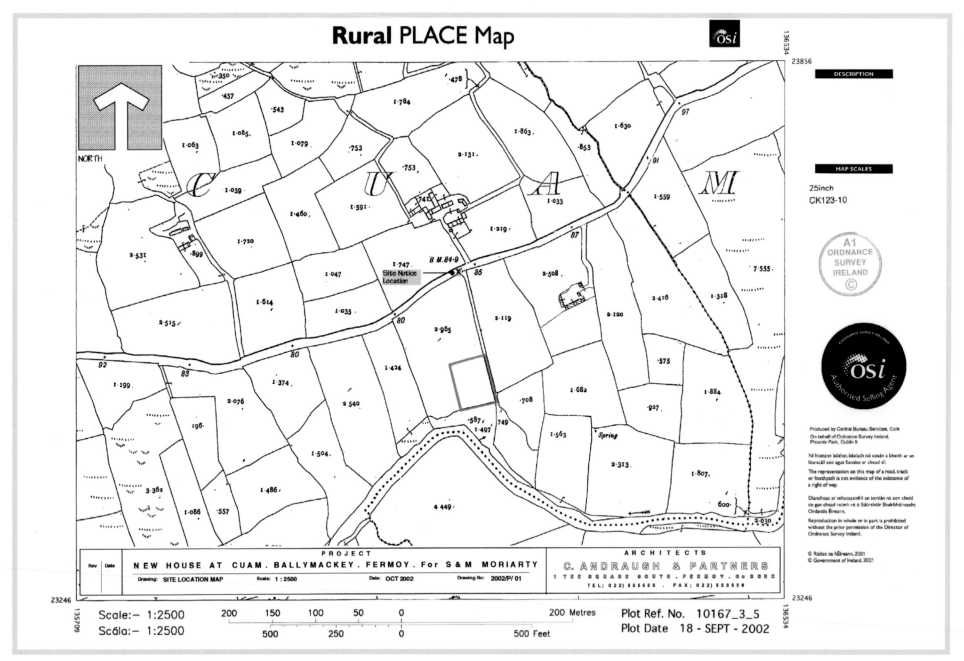

NORTH

23856

DESCRIPTION

MAP SCALES

25inch
CK123-10

A1
ORDNANCE
SURVEY
IRELAND
©

OSi
Authorised Selling Agent

Produced by Central Bureau Services, Cork
On behalf of Ordnance Survey Ireland,
Phoenix Park, Dublin 8.

Ní hionann bóthar, béalach nó cosán a bheith ar an
léarscáil seo agus fianaise ar chead slí.

The representation on this map of a road, track
or footpath is not evidence of the existence of
a right of way.

Dlanchosc ar mhacasamhlí an iomlán ná aon chuid
de gan chead roimh ré ó Stiúrthóir Shuirbhéireacht
Ordanáis Éireann.

Reproduction in whole or in part is prohibited
without the prior permission of the Director of
Ordnance Survey Ireland.

© Rialtas na hÉireann, 2001
© Government of Ireland, 2001

Site Notice Location

Spring

PROJECT
Rev | Date
NEW HOUSE AT CUAM. BALLYMACKEY. FERMOY. For S & M MORIARTY
Drawing: SITE LOCATION MAP   Scale: 1 : 2500   Date: OCT 2002   Drawing No: 2002/P/ 01

ARCHITECTS
C. ANDRAUGH & PARTNERS
1 THE SQUARE SOUTH . FERMOY . Co CORK
TEL; 022) 555555 . FAX; 022) 555556

23246

23246

Scale:— 1:2500   200 150 100 50 0   200 Metres
Scála:— 1:2500   500 250 0   500 Feet

Plot Ref. No.   10167_3_5
Plot Date   18 - SEPT - 2002

(planning application contents)

CORK COUNTY COUNCIL
COMHAIRLE CHONTAE CHORCAÍ

PLANNING APPLICATION FORM

For office use only	
Receipt No.	
Cash/ Cheque	
Date	
Plan. Ref. No.	

Type of Permission Sought

A. **Permission** ✓

B. **Permission for Retention**

C. **Permission consequent on the Grant of Outline Permission**

In the case of C above, please state Planning Authority Register Reference Number and date of grant of outline permission _____

PART 1 — DETAILS OF APPLICANT(S)

(i) Name of Applicant(s) — SEAN & MARY MORIARTY

(ii) Address of Applicant — CUAM, BALLYMACKEY FERMOY

(iii) Correspondence Address — C/o C. ANDRAUGH & PARTNERS N° 1 TEE SQUARE SOUTH FERMOY

(iv) Telephone No. **022-555555** Fax. No. **022-555556** E-Mail **cam@draw.net**

(v) If Applicant is a company -
(a) Name of Company Directors — N/A

(b) Registered address of company and Reg. No.

(c) Date of Incorporation

(vi) Name of person acting on behalf of applicant
(a) Address — C. ANDRAUGH & PARTNERS N° 1 TEE SQUARE SOUTH FERMOY

(b) Telephone No. **SEE ABOVE** Fax. No. **ditto** E-Mail **ditto**

(ix) State name, address and telephone number of person who prepared plans and drawings. — AS ITEM (VI) ABOVE

Andrew Pencil.

pp **C. ANDRAUGH & PARTNERS**
Signature of person acting
on behalf of applicant

ARCHITECT
B ARCH MRIAI
Qualification

7/R/2002
Date

M Moriarty
Signature of applicant

8 NOV 2002
Date

PART 2 — DETAILS OF PUBLIC NOTICES AND FEE

1. Newspaper notice
   (i) Name of newspaper — IRISH EXAMINER
   (ii) Date of publication — 7. 11. 2002

2. Date on which Notice was erected on site — 8. 11. 2002

3. The amount of fee enclosed and the basis for calculation — € 65

PART 3 — DETAILS OF PROPOSED DEVELOPMENT

4. Nature and extent of development — CONSTRUCT 2 STOREY HOUSE + INSTALL SEPTIC TANK

5. Location, townland or postal address of land or structure concerned — CUAM, BALLYMACKEY FERMOY

6. Did you have formal pre-planning discussions regarding this development?
   If so, please state with whom and date — Yes ✓ No
   JANE FINCH AREA PLANNER 2 OCT 2002

7. Interest in land or structure (please tick appropriate box)
   (a) Owner — Yes _____ No _____
   (b) Leasee — Yes _____ No _____
   (c) Contracted to Purchase — Yes ✓ No _____

8. Date of Purchase, if applicable — 13 MAY 2002

9. Name and address of owner (If not applicant) — TED BROWN CUAM, BALLYMACKEY

Where the application relates to a building or buildings indicate :-
(i) Gross floor space of building(s) in sq.m. : — 216 M²
(ii) Gross floor space of building(s) existing on site, if any, in sq. m. — NONE
(iii) The number of houses (if any) to be provided — 1 N° HOUSE

10. (i) Description of buildings and materials used in them:-

	Nature	Colour
(a) Floors	CONC/TIMBER	
(b) Walls and partitions	BLOCKW'K / TIMBER	
(c) Roof	SLATE ON TIMBER	

(ii) Nature and colour of proposed external facing materials:-

(a) Roofs	BLUE BLACK SLATE	
(b) Front Walls	PAINTED PLASTER + TIMBER	
(c) Side Walls	" "	
(d) Rear Walls	" " " "	
(e) Road boundary walls	SOD + STONE WALL	
(f) Other boundary walls	EXISTING + NEW HEDGEROWS	
(g) Buildings other than main buildings	N/A	

11. If application is for extension to dwelling, is it intended to use same as separate dwelling unit/granny flat. (If so, fee of €65 is payable)   Yes _____ No **✓**
Note : This must also be stated in Press Notice and Site Notice

12. If permission is granted do you intend to: ✓ as appropriate
Note : If the use is for short term/holiday letting, This must be stated in the Press Notice and Site Notice and the commercial rate of fee is applicable For each sq.m.

✓	Sell the house/site
	Use the house as your permanent house for year round occupation
	Let the house long-term
	Let the house short-term
	Use as a second home/holiday home
	Other : _____

_____
_____
(Please state intended use)

13. For applications for material change of use or for the retention of any such material change of use, please state
   (a) The existing use
   (b) The proposed use
   (d) Nature and extent of any such proposed use

   N/A
   _____
   _____
   _____

14. State special reasons (if any) for the selection of this particular site.

   IN FAMILY OWNERSHIP

15. Has planning permission been obtained on site in last 5 years. If so, please quote Register No.(s).

   NO

16. Is the development of a class prescribed in Schedule **5** to the Planning Regulations, 2001 requiring the preparation of an Environment Impact Statement?
   (If yes, an EIS should accompany this application)   Yes _____ No **✓**

17. Is the Development within a Strategic Development Zone?   Yes _____ No **✓**

18. Is the development located on land zoned residential or residential and other uses or within the development boundaries of towns and villages as zoned in the County Development Plan?   Yes _____ No **✓**

   If yes, please submit one of the following :

   (a) a copy of the certificate granted under section 97 of the 2000 Act exempting the applicant from the Housing Strategy's Scheme for Social and Affordable Housing Under Part V of the Act.
   (b) If a Certificate has not been issued, a copy of the application for same under Article 48 of the 2001 regulations.
   (c) Your proposals for compliance with any conditions which may be attached by the Planning Authority under Section 96(2) requiring the provision of housing referred to in section 94(4)(a) (Social and Affordable Housing).

19. Does the development consist of or comprise the carrying out of works to
   (a) a Protected Structure   Yes _____ No **✓**
   (b) a proposed Protected Structure   Yes _____ No **✓**
   Or to the exterior of a structure which is in
   (a) an architectural conservation area or   Yes _____ No **✓**
   (b) an area specified as such in a draft of a proposed Development Plan or   Yes _____ No **✓**
   (c) a proposed variation of a Development Plan   Yes _____ No **✓**
   Note : If yes to any one of the above, application must be accompanied by such photographs, plans and other particulars as are necessary to show how the proposed development would affect the character of the structure.

PART 4	DETAILS OF SITE AND SERVICES

20. (a) Acreage of Site   (a) **0.5 ACRES**
   (b) Length of road frontage   (b)
   52M (LANEWAY)

21. Distance of proposed building(s) from existing building :
   (a) On either side   (a) **125M TO EAST**
   (b) At front or rear   (b) **164M TO NORTH**

22. Size and description of drains (plans must show size and gradient) :   **100mm ⌀ @ FALL 1:60**

23. Description of connection drain to main and point of junction of drain with main. If septic tank is proposed, distances from proposed structures, public road and adjacent dwellings or structures and their respective septic tanks and bored wells, if applicable. These must be shown on the required 1/500 layout.
   TO SEPTIC TANK INSTALLED PER SR6. 1991

24. How supplied with water?   **DEEP BORE WELL**

25. How do you intend to dispose of site surface water?   **TO SOAKAWAYS WITHIN SITE**

26. Have there been any previous permissions on this site within the last five years?   **NO**

COMHAIRLE CHONTAE CHORCAI

FORM A

SEPTIC TANK: Site Suitability Assessment Report

NOTE 1: The following assessment should be carried out in accordance with SR6 1991.

NOTE 2: The completion of this form does not guarantee compliance with SR6 1991. Your attention is drawn to the information requirements of Para 1.4 of the document.

NOTE 3: This form should be accompanied by a site layout drawing, scale 1:500 or 1:200, showing location of water table trial hole and percolation test hole and proposed location of structures on site, including driveways and car parking.

Applicant's Name: **SEAN & MARY MORIARTY**

Address: **CUAM , BALLYMACKEY, FERMOY**

Location of Site: **AS ABOVE**   OS Ref No: **CK 123 - 10**

Floor Area of House: **216 m²**   No. of Bedrooms: _____

Date of Inspection: **24 SEPT 2002**

Date tests carried out: **27 SEPT 2002** Weather: **DRY + WINDY**

1. VISUAL ASSESSMENT

- Does the development comply with the site sizes, density and distance requirements of SR6 1991? **YES**

- Are there any existing or proposed wells within 100m of the percolation area?
  YES - PROPOSED WELL FOR APPLICANT

  If yes; specify distance and show on 1:500 or 1:200 site layout drawing:
  36.5M - SEE SITE LAYOUT PLAN

- Description of Site: (C/F Para. 2.5.1 of SR6 1991)
  THE SITE IS GENTLY SLOPING TOWARDS THE RIVER AND APPEARS WELL DRAINED NATURALLY.

- Description of site vegetation (C/F Para. 2.5.2. of SR6 1991)
  SITE LOCATED WITHIN MEADOW WITH NO EVIDENCE OF RUSHES , IRISES, ETC WHICH INDICATE SUITABLE CONDITIONS FOR PERCOLATION

11. TRIAL HOLE ASSESSMENT (Water Table Test)

- Depth of Trial Hole: **2.2 m**

- Depth from ground level to surface of water after 48 hours **1.9 m**
  (If none state "none")

- Depth from ground level to surface of rock **NONE**
  (If none state "none")

- SOIL PROFILE

	Description	Colour/Texture	Depth
Topsoil	SANDY LOAM	MEDIUM/DARK BROWN CRUMBLY LIGHT TEXTURE	400 mm
Subsoil Layer 1	SANDY CLAY		
Subsoil Layer 2			
Subsoil Layer 3			

111. PERCOLATION TEST RESULTS

TEST HOLE	1	2	3	4
SATURATION TIME (minutes)	75	60	60	65
DROP IN WATER LEVEL (mm)	100	100	100	100
OBSERVATION TIME (minutes)	35	45	45	40
PERCOLATION VALUE (minutes/25mm)	8.75	11.25	11.25	10
WAS TEST REPEATED?	NO	NO	NO	NO
AVERAGE VALUE	10.3			
"T" VALUE	10.31			
LENGTH OF PIPING	36 m			

1V. OTHER INFORMATION/OBSERVATIONS

ALL VISUAL INDICATIONS OF THE SITE SUGGEST ITS SUITABILITY FOR THE INSTALLATION OF A PERCOLATION AREA, BOTH IN TERMS OF THE AREA OF LAND AVAILABLE, THE NATURAL VEGETATION & GENTLE SLOPE OF THE SITE.

I certify that I have assessed the above site in accordance with the procedures of SR6 1991 and that the above statements are true and accurate.

I further certify that the above site is suitable for septic tank development and conforms in all respects to the requirements of SR6 1991.

Name   JOE FAHEY
(Block Capitals)

Signed   Joe Fahey
          PP. CANDROUGH + PARTNERS
Qualifications
(Block Capitals)   Dip. Arch Tech (C.I.T.)

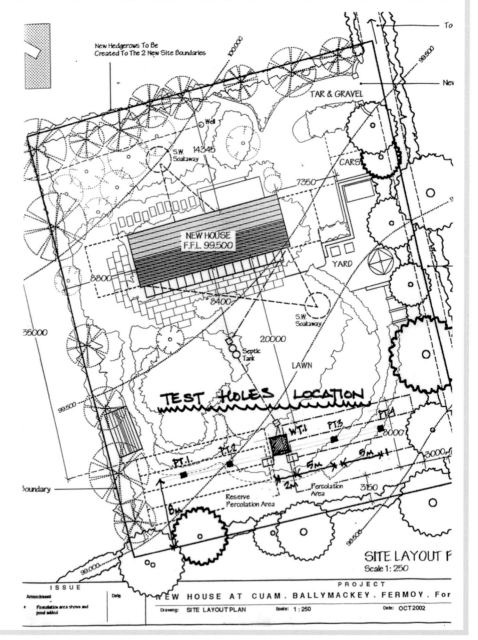

SITE LAYOUT P
Scale 1:250

ISSUE

Amendment

• Percolation area shown and pond added

PROJECT

NEW HOUSE AT CUAM. BALLYMACKEY. FERMOY. For

Drawing: SITE LAYOUT PLAN   Scale: 1 : 250   Date: OCT 2002

planning drawings

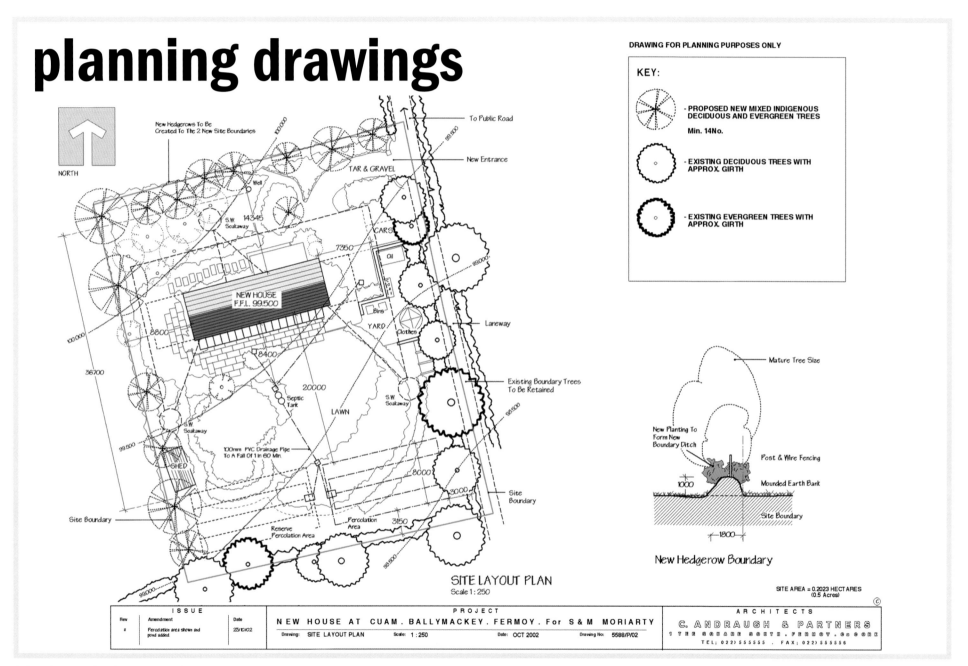

NORTH

New Hedgerows To Be Created To The 2 New Site Boundaries

To Public Road

New Entrance

TAR & GRAVEL

Well

S.W. 14345 Soakaway

7350

CARS

Oil

NEW HOUSE F.F.L. 99.500

Bins

Clothes

YARD

Laneway

8800

8400

Septic Tank

20000

LAWN

S.W. Soakaway

Existing Boundary Trees To Be Retained

36700

100.000

S.W. Soakaway

100mm PVC Drainage Pipe To A Fall Of 1 In 60 Min.

99.500

SHED

8000

Site Boundary

Site Boundary

3000

3150

Reserve Percolation Area

Percolation Area

99.000

SITE LAYOUT PLAN
Scale 1 : 250

KEY:

- PROPOSED NEW MIXED INDIGENOUS DECIDUOUS AND EVERGREEN TREES

  Min. 14No.

- EXISTING DECIDUOUS TREES WITH APPROX. GIRTH

- EXISTING EVERGREEN TREES WITH APPROX. GIRTH

Mature Tree Size

New Planting To Form New Boundary Ditch

Post & Wire Fencing

1000

Mounded Earth Bank

Site Boundary

1800

New Hedgerow Boundary

SITE AREA = 0.2023 HECTARES
(0.5 Acres)

ISSUE			PROJECT	ARCHITECTS
Rev	Amendment	Date	NEW HOUSE AT CUAM. BALLYMACKEY. FERMOY. For S & M MORIARTY	C. ANDRAUGH & PARTNERS
#	Percolation area shown and pond added	25/10/02	Drawing: SITE LAYOUT PLAN Scale: 1 : 250 Date: OCT 2002 Drawing No: 5588/P/02	1 THE SQUARE SOUTH. FERMOY. Co CORK TEL: 022) 555555 . FAX: 022) 555556

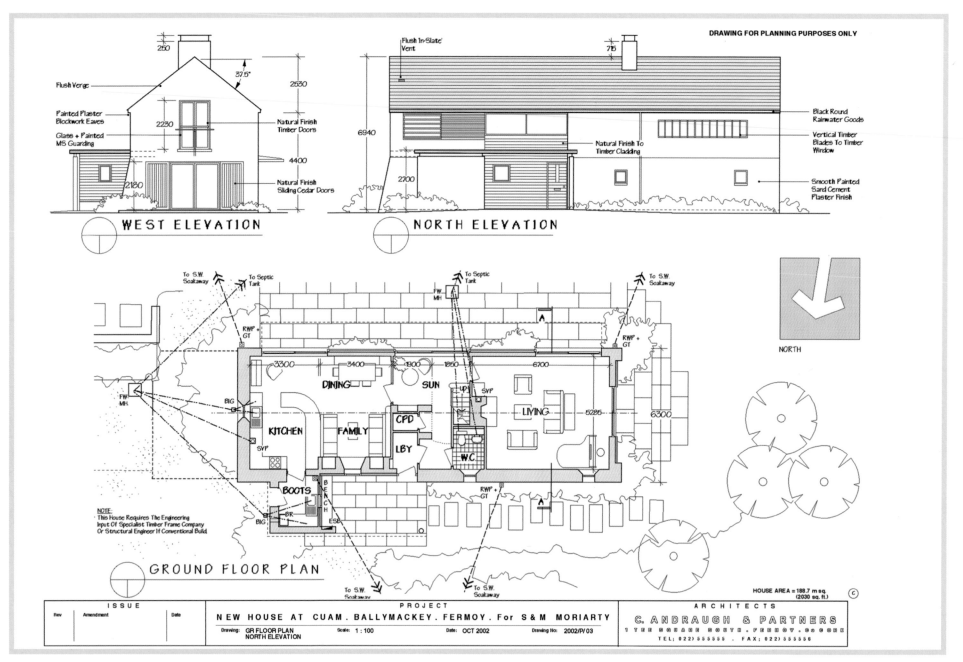

DRAWING FOR PLANNING PURPOSES ONLY

WEST ELEVATION

- Flush Verge
- Painted Plaster Blockwork Eaves
- Glass + Painted MS Guarding
- Natural Finish Timber Doors
- Natural Finish Sliding Cedar Doors
- 250
- 37.5°
- 2530
- 2230
- 4400
- 2180

NORTH ELEVATION

- Flush In-Slate Vent
- 715
- 6940
- 2700
- Natural Finish To Timber Cladding
- Black Round Rainwater Goods
- Vertical Timber Blades To Timber Window
- Smooth Painted Sand Cement Plaster Finish

GROUND FLOOR PLAN

- To S.W. Soakaway
- To Septic Tank
- To Septic Tank
- To S.W. Soakaway
- RWP + GT
- FW MH
- BIG
- KITCHEN
- SVP
- DINING
- FAMILY
- SUN
- CPD
- LBY
- WC
- LP
- SVP
- LIVING
- RWP + GT
- 3300
- 3400
- 1900
- 1850
- 6700
- 5285
- 6300
- BOOTS
- BENCH
- BR
- BIG
- ESB
- RWP + GT
- To S.W. Soakaway
- To S.W. Soakaway
- A
- A

NORTH

NOTE:
This House Requires The Engineering Input Of Specialist Timber Frame Company Or Structural Engineer If Conventional Build.

HOUSE AREA = 188.7 m sq. (2030 sq. ft.)

ISSUE			PROJECT	ARCHITECTS
Rev	Amendment	Date	**NEW HOUSE AT CUAM. BALLYMACKEY. FERMOY. For S & M MORIARTY**	**C. ANDRAUGH & PARTNERS**

Drawing: GR FLOOR PLAN NORTH ELEVATION Scale: 1 : 100 Date: OCT 2002 Drawing No: 2002/P/03

1 TEE SQUARE SOUTH . FERMOY . Co CORK
TEL: 022) 555555 . FAX: 022) 555556

116

(planning application contents)

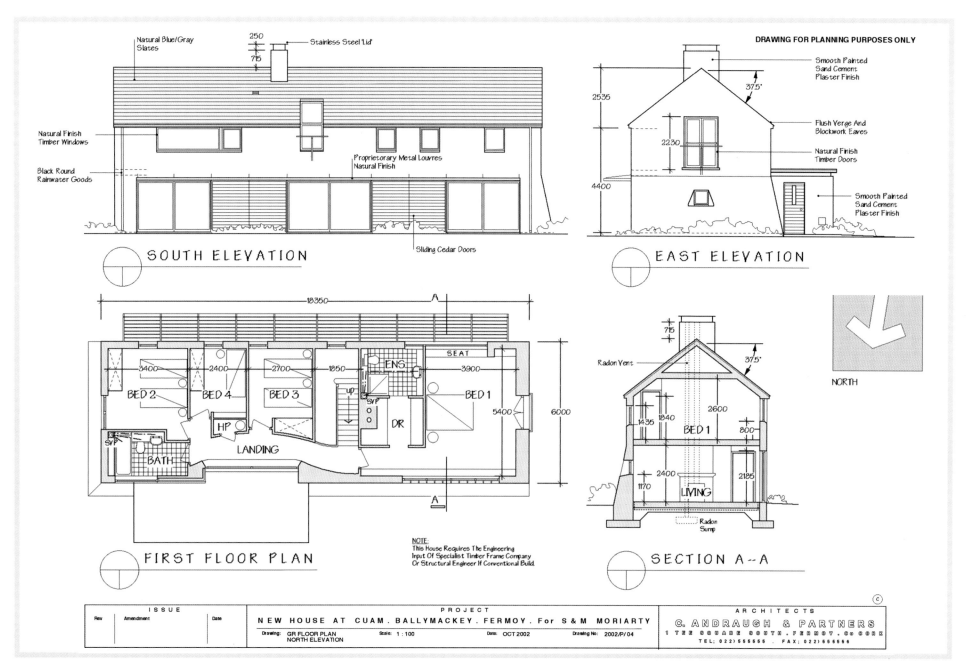

DRAWING FOR PLANNING PURPOSES ONLY

SOUTH ELEVATION

Natural Blue/Gray Slates
250
715
Stainless Steel 'Lid'
Natural Finish Timber Windows
Black Round Rainwater Goods
Proprietorary Metal Louvres Natural Finish
Sliding Cedar Doors

EAST ELEVATION

Smooth Painted Sand Cement Plaster Finish
375°
2535
2230
4400
Flush Verge And Blockwork Eaves
Natural Finish Timber Doors
Smooth Painted Sand Cement Plaster Finish

NORTH

FIRST FLOOR PLAN

18350
A
3400
2400
2700
1850
3900
SEAT
BED 2
BED 4
BED 3
ENS
BED 1
SVP
UP
HP
DR
SVP
LANDING
BATH
5400
6000
A

NOTE:
This House Requires The Engineering Input Of Specialist Timber Frame Company Or Structural Engineer If Conventional Build.

SECTION A--A

715
375°
Radon Vent
2600
1435
1840
BED 1
800
2400
2185
1170
LIVING
Radon Sump

	ISSUE		PROJECT	ARCHITECTS
Rev	Amendment	Date	NEW HOUSE AT CUAM. BALLYMACKEY. FERMOY. For S & M MORIARTY	G. ANDRAUGH & PARTNERS

Drawing: GR FLOOR PLAN NORTH ELEVATION   Scale: 1:100   Date: OCT 2002   Drawing No: 2002/P/04

1 THE SQUARE SOUTH. FERMOY. Co CORK
TEL; 022) 555555 . FAX; 022) 555556

checklist for planning applications

have you included:

Page of newspaper containing advert? ☐

Copy of the erected site notice? ☐

A plan showing the position of the site notice? ☐

6 copies of location map to a scale not less then 1:1250, identifying the site in colour and showing the level or contours of the land? (maps shall include Ordnance Survey sheet number, north point and scale & be of sufficient detail to enable ready identification of the site) ☐

A schedule listing all plans, maps and drawings? ☐

6 copies of the site suitability assessment report including test hole layout plan? ☐

6 copies of site layout plan at a scale not less than 1:500 showing adjoining land in blue and wayleaves in yellow; site boundary in red; identifying all buildings, roads, septic tanks, well stands of trees etc; marking distance of buildings from site boundaries? ☐

6 copies of drawings of floor plans of scale not less than 1:200, indicating dimensions and the name and address of person who prepared them? ☐

6 copies of drawings of all elevations of scale not less than 1:200, depicting dimensions and height of overall building and the name and address of the person who prepared them? ☐

The appropriate fee? ☐

appendices

Addressing the Deep Plan House

Trees and Shrubs

Bibliography

Picture and Design Credits

Acknowledgements and Accreditation

addressing the deep plan house an interpretation of the guide by

Mary Kerrigan Frank Harkin Architects and Project Management

In order to augment the design guidance within the document, CBP commissioned an architectural practice from outside the Cork region to interpret the guidance material, with the specific objective of addressing the very difficult design challenge of the deep plan two storey rural house. Mary Kerrigan Frank Harkin Architects, a registered practice with the RIAI with a track record of producing innovative and contemporary interpretations of the Irish rural house, was directed to develop one possible design approach to address the big box effect of the double deep plan, interpreting the guidance offered in the document on issues of scale, form, proportion, finishes etc. The practice was directed to work to a plan depth of nine metres accommodating a full two storey house and conservatory. Worked up sketches of both a two storey and a one and a half storey interpretation of the double deep plan house are featured overleaf.

This solution offers a fusion between the traditional and the contemporary as an adaptation of the rectangular box plan. Efforts have concentrated on achieving a less dominant primary roof form that is in harmony with the scale and proportions of the traditional farmhouse. This has been achieved by setting the horizontal external gable dimension at 7.5m with a 37.5° double pitched roof. The additional internal floor area has been achieved by adding a contemporary interpretation of a rear "lean-to". By handling this element in a very contemporary manner it is possible to marry a flat roof (either finished in lead or pvc membrane) with the traditional form of the rest of the house. The introduction of this contemporary intervention offers the opportunity for the rear wall to be treated entirely differently from the rest of the house both in terms of finishes and relationship of solid to void. **Whilst shown below as a two storey option, the same house can easily be applied to the storey and a half with no change to the footprint. This is depicted on the opposite page as a storey and a half incorporating a contemporary reinterpretation of the eaves dormer.**

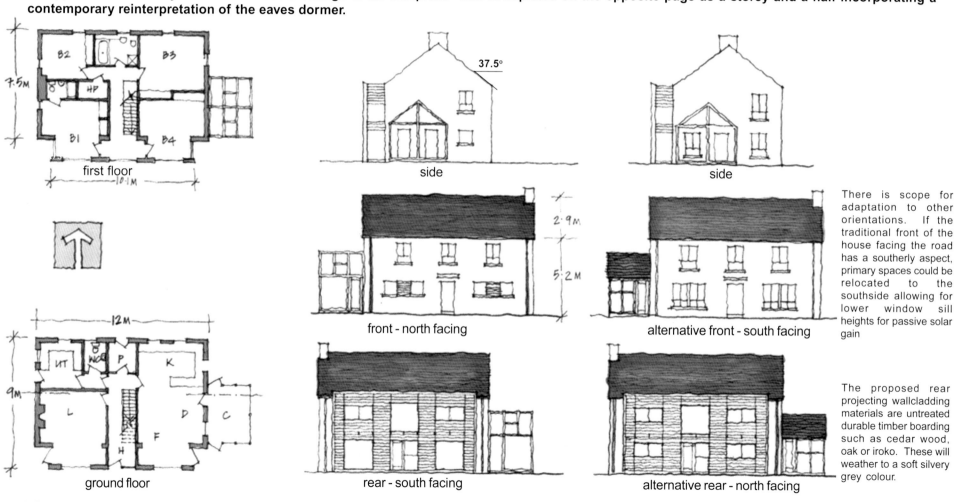

first floor

side

side

front - north facing

alternative front - south facing

rear - south facing

alternative rear - north facing

ground floor

There is scope for adaptation to other orientations. If the traditional front of the house facing the road has a southerly aspect, primary spaces could be relocated to the southside allowing for lower window sill heights for passive solar gain

The proposed rear projecting wallcladding materials are untreated durable timber boarding such as cedar wood, oak or iroko. These will weather to a soft silvery grey colour.

2 Storey House - 186 m² or (2000 sq ft) plus conservatory

© Mary Kerrigan Frank Harkin Architects and Project Management

The use of a flat roof to help achieve the depth in the plan form, whilst retaining a 37.5º roof pitch, is a challenging concept not to be deployed lightly in everyday commissions. Indeed, planners within the County will in most instances recommend great caution in their use, unless they can be demonstrated by a skilled hand, as in this case, to be an integral part of the design solution. Careful detailing is critical to their success as a design element. Where such an element cannot be handled skillfully, designers should revert to the more conventional design solutions advised for the deep plan form, illustrated on pages 66 and 67 of the document.

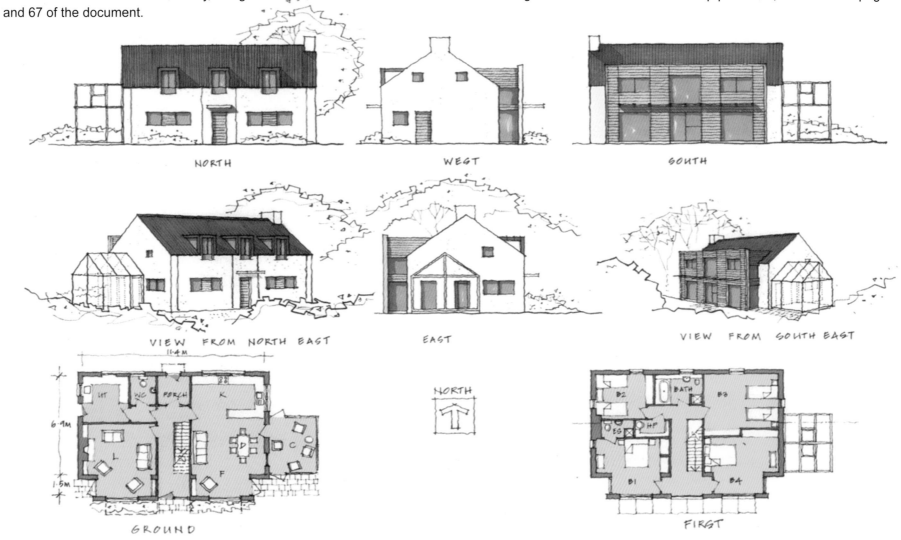

NORTH   WEST   SOUTH

VIEW FROM NORTH EAST EAST VIEW FROM SOUTH EAST

NORTH

GROUND   FIRST

*for alternative solutions to the deep plan house see pages 66 and 67

new boundary planting

Below is a list of trees and shrubs suitable for countryside hedgerows and shelterbelts. This list is not exhaustive, but gives an indication of some of the appropriate species to consider when planting for shelter. This list has been adapted from a similar one produced by Kerry County Council.

name	suitability	advantages	disadvantages
Alder *Alnus glutinosa*	Streamside, damp or waterlogged	Fast growing, easy to establish, good in clay,fill and wet soils	Will not flourish in stagnant water
Ash *Fraxinus excelsior*	Open woodland and hedgerows	Good in windswept, exposed and coastal sites	Will not grow in shade
Birch *Betula*	Good pioneer species, open and woodland sites	Good in damp and poor soils, for sheltering slower growing species.	
Blackthorn *Prunus spinosa*	Hedgerows, woods, banks and dense thickets	Good in stoney soils, windswept, exposed and coastal sites, stockproof	
Wild Cherry *Prunus avium*	Woods and hedgerows	Attractive blossom and foliage, easily established	
Crab Apple *Malus sylvestris*	Good in hedgerows	Attractive blossom, form and foliage, easily established	Requires open location
Elder *Sambucus nigra*	Good in hedgerows and woodlands	Fast growing, tolerates exposed conditions. Berries edible	
Elm *Uimus glabra*	Good in hedgerows and woodland	Fast growing, tolerates exposed conditions	Dislikes dry sites, prone to Dutch Elm disease
Gorse *Ulex europaeus*	Hedgerows and scrub	Evergreen, fast growing, good protection for saplings	
Guelder rose *Viburnum opulus*	Hedgerows and woodland edges	Attractive blossom, form and foliage	
Hawthorn *Crataegus monogyna*	Hedgerows and scrub	Good protection for saplings, deters livestock	Dislikes acid soils and wet sites
Hazel *Corylus avellana*	Hillsides, woodland understorey	Coppices easily, prevents erosion of thin, hillside soils	Dislikes acid soils
Holly *Ilex aquilifolium*	Woodlands	Evergreen, tolerant of exposure	Dislikes wet sites, difficult to establish
Honeysuckle *Lonicera periclymenum*	Climber good in hedgerows	Attractive flowers, hardy.	
Oak *Quercus*	Best on its own or in groups	Tolerates shallow, rocky soils, very windfirm	Needs shelter when young

Privet *Ligustrum vulgare*	Hedgerows	Easily established, attractive flowers	
Rowan (or Mountain Ash) *Sorbus **aucuparia***	Woodlands, hillsides	Hardy, tolerant of exposure, attractive flowers and berries	Prefers dry sites
Whitebeam *Sorbus Intermedia*	Woodland, rocky ground	Tolerant of coastal exposure, attractive foliage and flowers	As Rowan but better tolerance of damp soils
Willow *Salix*	Stream sides and damp sites	Fast growing, good shelter and screen trees	Cannot survive permanent waterlogging

non-native trees(introduced naturalised species)

Beech *Fagus sylvatica*	Single trees, shelter belts	Salt tolerant, will grow in shade	Grows best when 'nursed'
Fuschia *Fuschia magellanica*	Good in hedgerows	Attractive flowers and foliage	
Larch *Larix*	Single trees and plantations	Deciduous, conifer, withstands exposure, deep rooted	
Lime *Tilia vulgaris*	Single trees, woodland	Attractive form	Needs shelter when young
Horse Chestnut *Aescus hippcastanum*	Woodland, single trees	Attractive form, flowers and autumn colour	
Sweet chestnut *Castanae sativa*	Woodland	Fast growing, easily coppiced	Suffers from cold and exposure

conifers

Scots Pine *Pinus sylvestris*	Single trees and groups	Attractive foliage, good on dry, rocky and acid soils	Dislikes lime and wet peat
Corsican Pine (or Black Pine) *Pinus nigra*	Single trees and groups	Good shelterbelt, salt tolerant, good on limestone and sand	Not windfirm on clay
Juniper *Juniperis communis*	Single trees and groups	Open moorland and chalky soils, good shelterbelt. Edible berries.	
Lodge Pole Pine *Pinus contorta*	Windswept areas	Fast growing, very tolerant, good on damp soils	
Yew *Taxus baccata*	Single trees and groups	One of the first trees to bloom each year	

124

bibliography

Aalen *et. al.*(eds.) (1998), Atlas of the Irish Rural Landscape Cork University Press

An Taisce, Housing in West Cork –Design Guidelines, 1995

Association for the Protection of Rural Scotland (1997) Changing places -The Design and Siting of Housing in Rural Scotland

Becker, A, Olley, J, Wang, W (1997) 20th Century Architecture Ireland, Prestel

Borders Regional Council (1993), New Housing in the Borders Countryside, Policy and Guidance Note December 1993, Planning and Development Department.

Brecon Beacons National Park Committee (1988), Building Design: A Guide for Developers, Brecon Beacons National Park, Wales

Chandler, R, Doyle, D, Gibney, A, McDonnell, R and O'Regan, A (1980) The Roadstone Book of House Designs, Roadstone Ltd.

Council for the Protection of Rural England (1996), Local Attraction: the design of new housing in the countryside CPRE, London

Department of the Environment of Northern Ireland (1994), A Design Guide for Rural Northern Ireland, Town and Country Planning Service, Belfast: HMSO

Department of the Environment Northern Ireland, Dwellings in the Mournes: a Design Guide, DoE Countryside and Wildlife Branch, Belfast

Earley, J MSc (1998) Trees and Hedgerows, Cork County Council

Essex Planning Officers Association (1997), The Essex Design Guide for Residential and Mixed Use Areas, Essex County Council, England

Fladmark, J.M., Mulvagh, G.Y. & Evans, B.M.(1991), Tomorrow's Architectural Heritage –landscape and buildings in the countryside, Mainstream Publishing Company (Edinburgh) Ltd

Fladmark, J.M., Hill, B.M. & Donald, J (1994), Landscape & Architecture: Basic Design for Decision Makers, Scottish Natural Heritage and Scottish Homes (draft)

Galway County Council Design Guidelines for the Single Rural House - Appendix to the County Development Plan 2003-2009

Geoghegan, Philip and Delphine (1997), Building Sensitively and Sustainably in County Louth: landscape, settlement and building tradition, Louth County Council, (Published by Louth County Council as a support and clarification of the policies for housing location in the County Development Plan, 1997).

Geoghegan, Philip and Delphine (1997), Design Guidelines for Single Houses in the Countryside, Louth County Council

Harper, P, Light, J, Masden, C (1994), The Natural Garden Book: Gardening in Harmony with Nature Gaia Books Ltd.

Kerry County Council, Building in Rural Areas - Appendix H to the Kerry County Development Plan

McCullough, N and Mulvin,V (1987), A Lost tradition: the Nature of Architecture in Ireland, Gandon Editions Dublin

Moray District Local Plan 1993-1998: Housing in the Countryside, Moray District Council, Scotland

Naismith, Robert J. (1989), Buildings of the Scottish Countryside, Countryside Commission of Scotland, Victor Gallancz, London

Ni Lamhna, E (2002), Talking Wild, Town House and Country House Ltd

Peak National Park (1987), Building Design Guide

Perth and Kinross District Council (1995), Guidance on the Siting and Design of Houses in Rural Areas

Roche, N. (1999), The Legacy of Light - a History of Irish Windows, Wordwell Ltd.

Rothery, S. (1997) The Buildings of Ireland, The Lilliput Press Ltd.

Royal Incorporation of Architects in Scotland (1993), Fields of Vision – New Ideas in Rural House Design, RIAS Edinburgh

Shaffrey, Patrick and Maura (1985) Irish Countryside Buildings - everyday architecture in the rural landscape, O'Brien Press Dublin

The Scottish Executive (1991), Designing Places: a policy statement for Scotland

The Scottish Office (1991), Siting and Design of New Housing in the Countryside, PAN 36, HMSO, Edinburgh

The Scottish Office (1994), Fitting New Housing Development into the Landscape, PAN 44, HMSO, Edinburgh

The Scottish Office (1998), Investing in Quality: improving the design of new housing in the Scottish Countryside (a consultation paper)'

UCD School of Architecture, Building Sensitively in Ireland's Landscapes, prepared by the Housing and Urban Design Research Institute, published by Bord Failte, An Taisce & Galway County Council

Irish Architecture Journals and Annuals and various publications by the RIAI

photo & design credits

photo credits

colin buchanan and partners ltd
Photographs
4, 5, 6, 7, 17, 18, 19, 20, 23, 28, 29, 30, 37, 54,60, 61, 62, 63, 65, 66, 68, 91, 93, 95, 99,105, 106, 107, 108, 109, 110, 111, 112, 113, 119, 122, 129, 135, 136, 162.

mike shanahan + associates, architects
Photographs
1, 2, 3, 10, 11, 12, 13, 15, 21, 22, 24, 25, 26, 27, 31, 32, 33, 34, 35, 36, 40, 42, 44, 45, 46, 47, 48, 50, 51, 52, 53, 55, 56, 57, 58, 59, 64, 67, 69, 70, 71, 72, 73, 74, 75, 76, 77, 88, 89, 90, 92, 94, 96, 97, 98, 100, 114, 115, 116, 117, 118, 120, 121, 123, 124, 125, 126, 127, 128, 130, 131, 133, 134, 137, 138, 139, 140, 141, 142,143,145, 146,147, 148, 149, 150, 151, 152, 153, 155, 156, 157, 158, 159, 160, 161, 163, 164, 165,167,168,169,170,172,173,174,175.

design credits - houses featured

Every effort has been made to credit correctly the houses which appear in the Guide. Any omissions or inaccuracies should be brought to the attention of the Planning Policy Unit, details at front.

1	Niall Hyde Architect
8	John Dorman Architects (Photo courtesy of John Dorman Architects)
9	Michael Williams Associates (Photo courtesy of Michael Williams Associates)
11	Donal Hoare Architect
14	Simon Conolly, Akiboye Conolly Architects (Photo courtesy of Akiboye Conolly Architects)
15	SSA Architects
16	Tony Kelly, Wilson Architecture (Photo courtesy of Wilson Architecture)
17	D. Anderson, Diamond Redfern Anderson
22	W. Sutchbury (Extension)
24	Donal Hoare Architect
26	SSA Architects
29	Caroline Dickson Architects
33	Niall Hyde Architect
34	SSA Architects
38	Jim Horan, O'Dowd O'Herlihy Horan Architecture (Photo courtesy of O'Dowd O'Herlihy Horan Architecture)
39	Tom Hegarty, O'Riordan Staehli Architects
40	W. Stutchbury, SSA Architects
41	Pat McCabe, Simon J Kelly + Partners (Photo courtesy of Simon J Kelly + Partners)
42	Peter Lundqvist Architect
43	Paul Leech, Gaia Ecotecture
44	MSA Architects

47   Niall Hyde Architect
48   MSA Architects
49   Pat McCabe of Simon J Kelly + Partners Architects (Photo courtesy of Simon J Kelly + Partners)
51   Kees van Dam Architect
53   Kees van Dam Architect
55   Nick & Elaine Brown Architects
59   Cork County Council Architects
78   Roisin Murphy, Warren Architecture and Interiors (Photo courtesy of Warren Architecture and Interiors)
79   Roisin Murphy, Warren Architecture and Interiors (Photo courtesy of Warren Architecture and Interiors)
80   Pat McCabe, Simon J Kelly + Partners Architects (Photo courtesy of Simon J Kelly + Partners Architects)
81   Paul Keogh, Paul Keogh Architects
82   Shelley McNamara & Yvonne Farrell, Grafton Architects
83   Prof Kulka and Daly Barry Associates (Photo courtesy of Daly Barry Associates)
84   Mary Kerrigan Frank Harkin Architects and Project Management (Photo courtesy of Mary Kerrigan Frank Harkin Architects and Project Management)
85   Michael Williams Associates (Photo courtesy of Michael Williams Associates)
86   Mary Kerrigan Frank Harkin Architects and Project Management (Photo courtesy of Mary Kerrigan Frank Harkin Architects and Project Management)
87   Tony Kelly, Wilson Architecture (Photo courtesy of Wilson Architecture)
94   OPW Architects
98   Geoffrey Bainister Architect
101   Tom Hegarty, O'Riordan Staehli Architects
102   Tom Hegarty, O'Riordan Staehli Architects
103   Tom Hegarty, O'Riordan Staehli Architects
104   Prof Kulka and Daly Barry Associates
105-113 D. Anderson, Diamond Redfern Anderson
114   Donal Hoare Architect
119   Orna Hanly Architects
120   D.Anderson, Diamond Redfern Anderson
121   MSA Architects
123   Cork County Council Architects
125   OPW Architects (TBC)
129   Orna Hanly Architect
130   D.Anderson, Diamond Redfern Anderson
131   unknown
132   Prof Kulka and Daly Barry Associates (Photo courtesy of Daly Barry Associates)
133   Cole Partnership
135   Caroline Dickson Architects
136   Orna Hanly Architect
137   Cork County Council Architects
138   Niall McLaughlin Architects
140   MSA Architects
141   WA Houlihan Architect
142   MSA Architects
143   D.Anderson, Diamond Redfern Anderson